REFLECTIONS FOR WOMEN ALONE

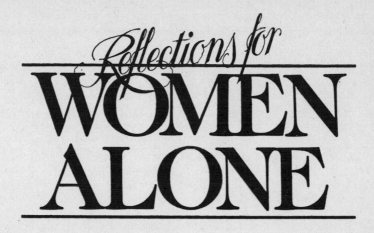

Reflections for WOMEN ALONE

CAROLE SANDERSON STREETER

VICTOR BOOKS ®
A Division of Scripture Press Publications Inc.

Scripture quotations from the *New English Bible* are © 1961, 1970, The Delegates of the Oxford University Press and the Syndics of the Cambridge University Press. Other Scripture quotations are from *The Modern Language Bible: The Berkeley Version in Modern English,* © 1945, 1959, 1969 by Zondervan Publishing House. Used by permission. Scripture quotations from *The New American Standard Bible* are © the Lockman Foundation 1960, 1962, 1963, 1968, 1971, 1972, 1973, 1975, 1977. Quotations from *The New King James Version* are © 1979, 1980, 1982, Thomas Nelson, Inc., Publishers. Other Scripture quotations are from *Weymouth's New Testament in Modern Speech,* by Richard Francis Weymouth—special arrangement with James Clarke & Company Ltd. Reprinted by permission of Harper & Row, Publishers, Inc.

Recommended Dewey Decimal Classification: 301.412

Suggested Subject Heading: SINGLE WOMEN

Library of Congress Catalog Card Number: 87-61506

ISBN: 0-89693-300-8

CONTENTS

PERSON

1

1. Single Reflections   11
2. God Knows Your Name   20
3. Great Expectations   27
4. "Jesus, You're Late!"   37
5. Stranger in My Mirror   44
6. The Mirror of Friendship   51
7. Too Much Effort   59

PLACE

2

8. A Place of Her Own   67
9. Cry Homeward   75
10. The Kingdom of Touch   83
11. The Silence of the Word   92
12. The Long Word   99
13. The House of Yesterday   107
14. The House in the Forest   115

PURPOSE

3

15. Setting Your Own Agenda   123
16. The Calling   129
17. Possessing the Possible   136
18. The Necessary Work   145
19. A Matter of Choice   152
20. Enlarging Your World   157
21. The Mirror of the Holy   167

PREFACE

We grow proportionate to our calling
as women who must not submit
to less than what was meant to be.

Your aloneness is a place that looks and feels like you, with
dimensions shaped around the contours of your soul. It is
good to examine the shape of your aloneness, for it has its
own personality which is formed in part from your needs.

This book deals with three of these most basic needs,
which came to my attention several years ago, during a
Sunday afternoon visit with my daughter, Catherine, on her
back porch in Chicago. She had graduated from college, was
recently married, and had begun working in her chosen
profession.

I asked her that day what made her feel significant as a
person. She thought a minute and then said, "I want someone to care about me, a place where I belong, and something
of value to do."

Catherine was not a woman alone. She was well on her way
to finding these basic needs fulfilled, and she felt high expectation for the future. And yet as I thought about her response,
I knew that the needs she expressed were mine and yours
and all of ours, for they are so deeply human.

Nor is that the end of Cathy's story, or yours and mine, as
if she has attained and we have not. For even as I have
watched her in these years reach for belonging and placing
and significance in what she does, I have been doing the
same thing myself, but in different ways. Although Cathy has
a loving husband and now a child, she too will feel days of
aloneness.

You and I who are lacking the special someone—what of us? Certainly, there will be times of profound aloneness, but also times and places and people and experiences of high significance. For if we know in ourselves what we can become, we want to live out what we see within. And so we reach again for the challenge that is given, day by day.

Carole Sanderson Streeter
CAROL STREAM, ILLINOIS
1987

1

PERSON

1

SINGLE REFLECTIONS

There are no good women but only women who have lived under the influence of a good man.

Sir Almroth Wright

I know myself as I am known.
I see myself as by reflection,
in loving eyes, indifferent eyes, hating eyes,
all show me myself.

But what I am to be is seen by love alone.
For only love can find the way
past this day's limitations,
confidently grasp the sureness of tomorrow.

CSS

When Eve wanted to see a reflection of her face, she would have looked into a pool of water, perhaps into one of the rivers that slowly wended through the Garden. But when Eve wanted to see what she was to another human being, she would have looked at Adam, for in his eyes, she would have seen the most accurate reflection of herself—bone of my bone, flesh of my flesh.

When *you* want to see a reflection of your face, you hold up a looking glass. When you want to see your value to another human being, where then do you look? To a parent, friend, child or grandchild, a sister or brother? But it's not the same, is it?

According to a survey of 4,900 women conducted for *Working Woman* magazine, and published in early 1985, "the women who are most satisfied with their lives—whether or not they are mothers—are married. Next come women who are living with someone, then the never-married, and last, those who have been divorced."[1]

That's not surprising. I believe that most women experience the unmarried state as unnatural, as something other than what they were made for. While this feeling may reflect the expectations of society or the wishes of family, it is more than this, for most unmarried women know in themselves that something is missing.

How else do we explain a society so bent on marrying? Even with the divorce rate for first marriages at about fifty percent, once-divorced people are not discouraged from trying again, and within five years after divorce, eighty-five percent of them remarry. Sixty percent of the second marriages fail, and yet seventy-five percent of those people marry yet a third time.[2]

This is all somewhat astonishing, especially with the multiple families created, the confused kinship, the loosened loyalties. In 1986, there were fifty million people in blended families in the United States. Some family counselors say it takes four to five years for children to adjust to the second family, and even longer for adults.

Many younger people who sought solace yet freedom in living together without marriage found that it was not enough. They discovered that they had to be married to express their commitment and love. How do we explain all of this? What do women want, that keeps them marrying or wanting to marry?

What Do Women Want?

This ever-current question is the theme of a centuries-old story in which a knight was sent out by the queen to discover the answer, on peril of his life. He found some answers that were true enough, but none that were true for enough women. You may recognize this story as the "Wife of Bath's Tale" in

Chaucer's *Canterbury Tales*. When the knight traveled the countryside in pursuit of an answer,

> Some said, "Fair fame."
> Some said, "Prettiness."
> Some said, "Rich array."
> Some said, "Lust abed and often to be widowed and re-
> wed."
> Some said, "Our poor hearts are aye most eased when we
> have been most flattered and thus pleased."
> Some said, "We do love the best to be quite free to do our
> own behest and that no man reprove us for our
> vice, but saying we are wise, take our advice."
> Some said, "Great delight have we to be held constant, also
> trustworthy, and on one purpose steadfastly to
> dwell."

All of these replies, while true in their way, left the knight unsatisfied. Then he met an ugly old woman, "a fouler person could no man devise," who offered him the right answer in exchange for his promise that he would do for her whatever she asked. He agreed, since he was dead anyway if he didn't find the answer. He traveled back to court, with her at his heels, to be sure she got her end of the bargain. The reply he gave to the queen was this:

> "My leige lady, generally," said he,
> "Women desire to have the sovereignty
> As well upon their husband as their love,
> And to have mastery of their man above;
> This thing you most desire, though me you kill;
> Do as you please, I am here at your will."
> In all the court there was no wife or maid
> Or widow that denied the thing he said.

For her trouble, the old woman wanted that he take her to wife, and over great restraint on his part, he finally

> Was so constrained that he needs must go and wed,
> And take his ancient wife and go to bed.

Once there, she talked to him with great persuasion on the meaning of a true gentleman, and how gentility comes from

God alone. He at last gave in and said to her,

"My lady and my love, and wife so dear,
I put myself in your wise governing;
Do you choose which may be the more pleasing,
And bring most honor to you, and me also.
I care not which it be of these things two;
For if you like it, that suffices me."

When she realized that she had the mastery over him, she turned into a beautiful young woman, and he saw that he now had all he had ever wished for. In his joy, "his heart bathed in a bath of utter bliss." From that time on, "she obeyed his wish in everything that might give pleasure.

The tale ends with a prayer that Jesus will send meek husbands to all women and give the women strength to outlive their husbands.[3]

Need for Significance

What do women want? When I hear some say that all they want is to be married, I am not convinced. We all are complex enough that we want many things in life; sometimes we want one good to achieve another.

However, beneath most of our desires is a need for significance. We want to matter, to figure in the scheme of things. Women traditionally have found the path to significance through influence over a man or men. While desires for beauty and fame, money and physical satisfaction, flattery, freedom, and trust are factors in women's lives, I would guess that all of them together would not outweigh the desire to be significant. Usually, the way to matter to a man is to marry him. The way to have some influence is to be legally bound.

One woman, newly widowed for the second time, was already lamenting that she had now and then been "bad" to her husband. She said, "I only got that way when I felt I was losing control." She carried control so far as to bring a lawyer into the hospital room of her dying husband and force him to sign a new will that nullified the financial arrangements they had made when they married only a few years before.

How could a single woman ever match this kind of control? Fortunately, not many want to; they just want the possibility.

As women alone, we live out our singleness in society. I sometimes wonder if singleness itself is the worse evil to most women, or if it is rather the spoken and unspoken assumptions of their culture. Many women can deal fairly well with seeing single reflections in the mirror, but fail when it comes to other people seeing those same reflections.

The author of *Eminent Victorian Women* looks at the question "What is a woman?" and offers some of the contradictory answers from people of a century ago. Most of the conceptions of women were from eminent men of the time, and their definitions reflected the ways they wanted the women in their lives to relate to them. The quotation with which this chapter begins is one example.[4]

In his excellent book, *Daughters of the Promised Land*, Page Smith gives many sensitive observations about women, especially in his chapter, "The Nature of Women."[5] However much I like his words, though, I have to remember that they are not dealing with woman as an individual, but rather with woman as a member of society. And this is precisely where most women alone have their greatest problems in being unmarried. Their role in life is generally not judged as being significant. They may be attractive, do excellent work, be highly involved with people. But they lack one thing—the diamond of great price.

Dealing with the Dreaded

During the Christmas holidays of 1985, both *Dear Abby* and *Miss Manners* ran columns on the December tendency to round up the "strays," meaning the single women. An objectionable term, but graphic. For there are a good many married women who will not by choice entertain a single woman in their homes, except as an act of charity.

We might think that there would be greater social comfort for the Christian woman who wants to be part of a church fellowship, but generally this is not so. The exclusion of people who are not coupled has given rise to large groups of single adults in churches across the United States. I can't believe that all these people want to be segregated. However, they do need to belong somewhere.

A few years ago, *Moody Monthly* magazine ran a series of short articles about the place of women in the church. Some of them were very helpful. But one, by a well-known minister, left no room for me. I said to a friend, "According to him, I don't even exist." I can't say this bothers me, since he isn't all that high on my list either. But I don't like the feeling that we can in our words and actions—and in the name of Christ—annihilate whole groups of people because we don't favor their way of life or their marital status.

Yet, I do understand the human inclination to categorize. It is easier to deal with people by groupings, rather than as individuals. It demands less to talk of role functions than to appreciate individual strengths. Unmarried people do the same thing. We categorize groups we are not part of, people we are not friends with, activities we feel we can't join. Every time we do this, we are blurring the reflections of ourselves; we are distorting and causing confusion to ourselves.

Rae VanDorn was confronted with her unmarried state in an extreme setting. As a young missionary in a Muslim society where women have meaning only as they relate to men, she found that the foundation of her Contented Single State was crumbling. Over a period of several weeks, her inner confusion about herself as a woman increased, until she could hardly decide what to do on any given day. "One morning, I woke up and realized I was on my way to becoming a victim of The Dreaded." Then began the process of dealing with God about her singleness, at times praying that He would hurry and send a man along, at other times complaining that He had given her confused guidance. After she finished blaming God, she turned inward and abused herself emotionally. Between these extremes, she sometimes asked God to make her a *good* missionary, but not often.

Wanting a solution, Rae began to read biographies of single women missionaries, and found that while they didn't wallow in The Dreaded State, they didn't ignore it either. "They let Him lift them back into Contented Singleness. Sometimes they didn't let Him lift them right away, and sometimes He had to lift them again and again. . . . And they rejoiced in the calling God had given them and in the freedom their singleness gave them to carry out that calling."[6]

A British publication, *Third Way*, included an article in its July 1986 issue entitled "Going Spare?" about single people in the church. The author, Veronica Zundel, mentioned two of the greatest problems for Christian unmarried people, their invisibility and the uncertainty they feel about themselves. Invisibility means that

> whatever aspects of life are not mentioned in social contexts such as Parliament or the media, are not really "seen" or, if noticed, are not seen as important. . . . If we adapt this analysis to singleness, it is easy to see how the general trend of teaching on women assumes that their primary role is to be a wife and mother, and that all of them either are or hope to be such. . . . It is but a small step from "I am not acknowledged" to "I do not matter" or even "I do not exist." Guilt and lack of self-worth are likely concomitants, especially where being a woman is itself suspect, until under the control of a man . . . the single Christian woman looks in vain for a positive appreciation of her existence and value. Should she put her energies wholly into work, she is damned with faint praise as "a career woman" (translation: no man would have her, she's too strong-minded). Should she channel them into pursuing marriage as a career, she is condemned as a "husband-hunter."
>
> An ever-present question for the single person who has achieved a degree of individuation is: "Who do I belong to?" Finding one's own identity is not an end in itself, especially for the Christian; it is a necessary preliminary to relating and committing oneself to others. But commitment to friends or fellow church members is usually neither permanent nor explicit, and lacks the public recognition accorded to family ties.[7]

Reflections of Sexuality

One evening during the time I was writing this book, I was talking with three friends about the project. One of them, a pastor of a large church in middle America, told us a story about an encounter he had with a single woman of middle age who is disabled with a crippling disease. She shared with him that one of the most difficult aspects of being alone *and* disabled is that people do not see her as a sexual being. My pastor friend became aware that he too had treated her that way, as though she were "safe." It was so easy to regard her as a sexless being. And he was sorry that he had compounded her feelings of inadequacy by his mindless behavior.

I was glad he told us the story, for it reminded me that whatever our marital status, present or past, we want men to treat us as women, as creatures with the potential, at least, of being attractive. We do not want to be categorized as totally safe, even when we choose to behave in safe ways. We want recognition that human sexuality is much more than physical sexual encounter. We want to be sure that we are looking into our mirrors and seeing creatures who are every bit as much women as those who are married.

Toward Clearer Reflections

Part of our need for significance is our intense desire to be taken seriously. If other people do not take us seriously, we have a hard time doing so. Conversely, if we do not take ourselves seriously, it is unlikely that anyone else will either. Since change has to begin somewhere, let it begin with us.

Some years ago at a conference I was attending for work, there was to be a gathering of all the single people. A man told me I should go and "celebrate my singleness." I told him I didn't feel that way and wasn't going.

I have thought about his comment several times since that evening, and I still don't feel that singleness is anything to celebrate. Rather, I regard singleness as a resource to be used, as a way of life with certain possibilities that I would not have if I were married. They are not better than those offered to married people, just different. Part of being grown-up is to accept what I have and to use it as fully as I can.

This is much easier to say than do, and I had a hard time learning what this means in a practical way. We can't make singleness work for us unless we accept it; accepting it means that we see it as having some benefits, some value.

For me, the process of coming to value my singleness involved a long and detailed look at the elements of my life, to see what they meant. That process was not easy, for I had long ago bought into the cultural assumption that "married is better." But *better* wasn't the point in my examination of being alone. The point was to discover my resources.

I also had to look at the assumptions of society to ascertain what I was up against, to decide what I had to ignore, what I had to work around, what could work for me.

When we predetermine that our needs for love and place and valuable activity must be met through marriage, and that there will be no significant loving and belonging and contributing without marriage, we work against ourselves. We stifle our expectations. We close ourselves off from receiving good things. We gaze into the reflecting pool of life and muddy the waters, for we have decided what we must see before we even look. What we see, therefore, is doubly distorted. Not only is there no man, but there is a woman whom we have already condemned as inferior, unattractive, disadvantaged, disabled, and more.

She stands before God's mirror unseeing. For
within her mind exists an image of
herself, transfixed upon the looking glass,
with painful pride of one who has become
her all, her only possibility.

God does have a mirror in which we can see the only accurate reflection of who we are. But we will never see it as long as we carry in our minds what we have determined must be part of our lives.

We know we don't approach a tangible mirror with the expectation of seeing what is not there. Yet, all too often, we do approach the mirrors of our inner selves that way. However, just as we have learned to do this, we can unlearn it. We can look into our mirror and smile and be friendly to the person we see. We can decide to make the reflection even better next month and next year.

There has to be more to life than just waiting . . . waiting for someone who doesn't materialize.

2

GOD KNOWS YOUR NAME

We are all under the same mental calamity;
we have all forgotten our names.
We have all forgotten what we really are.

G.K. Chesterton

"Peace, Beaver," said Aslan. "All names
will soon be restored to their proper owners."

C.S. Lewis

Your given name is very personally yours. It is like a badge of
identification. It becomes even more important when a crisis
causes you to question where you fit in the places that were
once part of your world, but are now less friendly.

I experienced this many years ago when after a long marriage,
I suddenly found myself in the world of single women. Because
I came this route through a way that had always been unthinkable to me, divorce, and because some people were already
pronouncing the judgment of God on me, I went through a
time of questioning just how God saw me.

I came to the reassuring conclusion that God did not view me
primarily in a role function. To God I was a person, and this
meant He knew my name, my given name. He had always
known it, from before the foundation of the world. I was also
reminded that God had been there in all the difficult years
leading up to the final break and that He was not going to

withdraw His love now when I needed Him more than ever. If He understood before, He certainly did now.

There is a strong connection between personal identity and names. To the ancient Hebrew, names carried destiny and personality. A citizen of Israel always bore the name of his tribe and clan and family, as well as his given names. In a more modern setting, when we lived in Ecuador, we found that our official names were quite different than in the United States. My last name on a government document was my mother's maiden name. While not used in a social context, this official notation keeps alive family names that could be easily lost through marriage.

You and I love to be called by name, to be recognized for who we are, to be noticed, to be remembered. We like to see our names inscribed on sheepskins and diplomas and birthday cards. When a couple is expecting a baby, they spend months choosing just the right names for their progeny. I believe this fascination with names is something we have acquired from our Heavenly Father.

God seems to have a passion for names that predates people or trees or even an earth. The first record of His naming something in our world is in the first chapters of Genesis as He accomplished the work of each creation day. The light He called Day, the darkness He called Night. The vault over the earth He called Heaven and the waters He called Seas. The dry land was named Earth. And on each work He finished, God placed a label that read, *Good*.

Man was named Adam, and was placed in a garden called Eden, where two of the trees were named Tree of Knowledge of Good and Evil and Tree of Life. To Adam, God gave the delightful task of naming each creature He had made.

This penchant for naming didn't stop after Creation. For mankind has been naming things ever since—labeling, listing, outlining, grouping, subdividing, defining, cataloging the world. And now with the computer, the possibilities for cross-listing are endless. Jacques Ellul comments on this inclination to name things:

> To name someone or something is to show one's superiority over him or it. . . . Human sovereignty is due more to our

language than to our techniques and instruments of war. One can claim or believe himself to be free because of language. Naming something means asserting oneself as subject and designating the other as object. It is the greatest spiritual and personal venture.[1]

When it came to defining Himself to people, God was not content with one name. In the Old Testament, we find multiple primary names by which He was known. In the Bible, there are as many names or expressions for God as days in the year. For Christ alone, there are more than one hundred names or phrases that express who He is. The people of God are called by at least ninety different terms.

God sometimes showed His personal concern for individuals through changing their names. Abram was renamed as Abraham, and Sarai as Sarah. When the wily Jacob finally developed some character, God changed his name to Israel, Prince with God. Jesus met Simon and said, "You are Simon, but you will be Peter."

You and I were known by God before we existed in form. We read in the Scriptures that we were chosen in Christ before the foundation of the world. Before time and space, God knew your name, your possibilities. And that name and those possibilities are not tied to marital status.

God chose that the name of Christ would be the rallying point for all who believe, that we would be saved by faith in His name, that a proof of our salvation would be that we would confess His name.

One of the best parts of God's obsession with names is yet to come, and reminds me of my pre-Christmas stashing away of gifts for the family. In August of 1985, I traveled to England and brought back so many gifts that they didn't fit in the closet where I usually kept presents. Some large shopping bags from London and Bath stood behind the armchair in my bedroom until I wrapped Christmas gifts.

Somewhere God has a huge pile of white stones, one for each person who has ever believed. For on a day future, after He has written something special on your stone, Christ is going to place it in your hand and close your fingers over it, for the words will be for you alone, a name that only you and God will know.

This is no nickname, no family name, no Christian name. It is a name, a word, that is exactly identical with us, which coincides with us, which is us. We may almost say it is a word which God pronounced when He willed us into existence and which is us, as we are it. This name defines our absolute and unrepeatable uniqueness as far as God is concerned. No one can know the name, as no one can, in the last analysis, know anyone as God knows him; and yet it is out of this name that everything else comes that can be known about us.[2]

Pandita

A century ago, a young woman of high family in India made her first visit to England and the United States to study and to seek support for her work in India. The name by which she was known was Pandita Ramabai, but that was not her given name. Because of the brilliant education she received from her Brahmin father, a college of scholars, or pandits, in Calcutta conferred on her the name of Pandita, which means "learned." "The name stuck with her and set her apart as one who demonstrated the ability of women in India to learn and lead."[3]

Born in 1858, Pandita grew up in the forest of Gungamul, a remote plateau in southern India, where her father educated both his wife and child. "By the time she was twelve, she had committed to memory eighteen thousand Sanskrit verses with all their rich stores of knowledge and wisdom. She had also learned Marathi, into which she later translated the Bible, and acquired a knowledge of Kanarese, Hindustani and Bengalese, and four other languages."[4]

During the terrible famine of 1876–1877, Pandita's family was brought to poverty. She saw the awful sufferings of so many people and then watched her own parents and sister die. Wandering through India with her brother in search of spiritual peace, she went to a young people's meeting in Calcutta where she was introduced to Christ, "who knew no caste, who gave neither man nor woman dominion over the other, and who loved all, Jew and Gentile alike. In India at that time, women ranked no higher than pigs; but in Christ she found a reason for the education of women."[5]

It was about this time that she came before the college of pandits, who found that her learning was equivalent to theirs. Although she was only twenty years old, she set to work to raise the level of women in India, especially the widows, who were often burned on their husbands' funeral pyres.

For a time her brother worked with her, but his health had been weakened by years of privation and he soon died. She later married his best friend, but within nineteen months, her husband was also dead, leaving her with a daughter, Manorama, which means "heart's joy." Pandita was now one of the twenty-three million widows in India. She wrote at this time, "This great grief drew me nearer to God."

As she continued to travel and lecture on the importance of education for women, she felt a great desire to go to England. "The voice came to me as to Abraham. Throwing myself on God's protection, I went forth as Abraham, not knowing whither I went."[6] She studied in England and was also appointed professor of Sanskrit in Cheltenham Ladies College. The next year she was invited to America, where she became the first woman from India to receive the degree of Doctor of Medicine from the Women's Medical College in Philadelphia. Her book, *The High Caste Hindu Woman*, was published in 1887, and brought the first direct knowledge to American churchwomen of the life of women in India. As a result, the Ramabai Association was formed to provide education for child widows of India.

In 1888, Pandita returned to India to publish the account of her travels and to open a home for widows in Bombay. She called it Abode of Wisdom. As she learned more about the terrible plight of young widows, she determined to do yet more for the women of India, and purchased land for the Mukti Mission, the name meaning, "salvation." She soon had over two hundred girls, and the number grew rapidly because of another famine. During this time a great revival came to the area; hundreds were converted and baptized.

As the work expanded, she saw the need to train the young women in vocations. They could learn weaving, tin work, shoemaking, carpentry, printing, needlecrafts, and she taught many to become teachers. Each year new structures were added—a hospital, offices, a bakery, dormitories, and a church. When the church was finished, she had the following lines inscribed on the foundation stone:

Praise the Lord.
Not by might, nor by power, but by My Spirit, saith Jehovah of Hosts.
That Rock was Christ. Upon this Rock I will build My church; and the gates of hell shall not prevail against it.
Jesus
September 29, 1899

In 1907, Pandita decided to translate the Bible into Marathi, the language of the common people. First she had to learn Greek and Hebrew, a task she worked into all her other duties. In her last months, in 1922, as she was completing work on the proof for her translation, she became ill and knew that the end was near. She prayed that God would give her ten more days in which to complete the proofreading. "On April 5, 1922, when the last proof was read, she fell asleep, never to wake again."[7]

When missionary statesman Robert Hall Glover evaluated the contribution of Pandita Ramabai, he said that she was universally acknowledged to be the most distinguished woman in India, native or foreign. "Her death was noted in both the secular and the religious press the world around, and a host of her friends of every race deeply mourn her loss."[8]

Who Defines Us?
Pandita did not allow society to define who she was to be. In part from her earthly father, and in a fuller way from her Heavenly Father, she was able to see a reflection of who she could be and what she could do for others.

We too need to refuse to be defined solely by the world around us. God didn't fashion us that we might forever make excuses about why we can't do this or that. We too can act with courage and imagination and creativity that mirror the motives of the Eternal One toward His people.

God knows your name as it is. He knows your past and your future and your circumstances and your weaknesses and strengths. He knows all your excuses, all your fears. He knows if you blame Him for what has or has not happened to you. Christ in all ways identifies with the human condition, even to the point of questioning His Father, "Why have You abandoned Me?" This is one isolation we will never experience as He did.

On a day future, when we are given our white stones, we will understand much better what our lives were all about. On that day we will also receive other gifts, crowns, new clothes, fruit from the Tree of Life, special place near to God, manna to eat, position in the kingdom, and we will hear our names spoken before the angels in heaven.

George MacDonald, nineteenth-century English novelist and pastor, said that only when we *become* our name does God give us the stone with our name on it, for only then can we understand what the name signifies.

It is the blossom, the perfection, the completeness, that determines the name, and God foresees that from the first because He made it so; but the tree of the soul, before its blossom comes, cannot understand what blossom it is to bear and could not know what the word meant which, in representing its own unarrived completeness, named itself. Such a name cannot be given until the man *is* the name. . . . To tell the name is to seal the success—to say, "In thee also I am well pleased."[9]

I wonder what God will say when He announces my name. I wonder what will be written on my white stone. I have some ideas already, and am moving slowly but surely toward letting Him show me who I really am, right now and also in potential, as reflected in His Fatherlove.

So come to Him, our living Stone—
the Stone rejected by men
but choice and precious in the sight of God.
Come, and let yourselves be built,
as living stones, into a spiritual temple.[10]

3

GREAT EXPECTATIONS

Single women have a dreadful propensity for being poor, which is one very strong argument in favor of matrimony.

Jane Austen

There is an old Norwegian saying, "It takes only two to make a marriage—a willing young lady and her anxious mother." That was not true just in Norway. If you have read the novels of Jane Austen, you'll remember the role of the mothers in finding eligible suitors for their daughters. In *Pride and Prejudice,* Jane describes Mrs. Bennet this way: "The business of her life was to get her daughters married; its solace was visiting and news." The last chapter of the book begins, "Happy for all her maternal feelings was the day on which Mrs. Bennet got rid of her two most deserving daughters."

Becky Sharpe, the orphaned heroine of William Thackeray's *Vanity Fair,* laments her motherless state: "I am alone in the world. I have nothing to look for but what my own labour can bring me. . . . I must be my own mama."

In a more recent offering, *Hello Dolly!* we see the matchmaker of Yonkers and New York City at her charmingly efficient best. Dolly's business was to ensure that the young people were properly matched for life.

But who helps the young woman of today? Mother isn't supposed to appear anxious or try to arrange the marriage. Dolly is out of style. But the matchmaking business is very much alive. Instead of calling an ethnic Dolly, today's up-wardly mobile young person has a choice of any number of services, some highly personal, some very exclusive, others on video and available to anyone. Some operate through magazines, others on a face-to-face basis in church-related or special interest organizations.

Millions of younger adults cluster in settings where they hope they will meet the right people. One Saturday while I was writing this book, I had lunch with friends at a new restaurant on North Clark Street in Chicago. This is New Town, the center of Chicago Yuppiedom. After we ate, we walked for several blocks and mingled with the young people out in their summer Saturday threads.

The streets were lined with stores filled with the kinds of merchandise these affluent young people want. Crowded between stores was a new high rise apartment building adver-tising Luxury One Bedroom Apartments to be ready soon. Buying is an important part of the lives of young adults, and many choose to live in neighborhoods of stores and in warm weather to eat in sidewalk cafes right on the street. James Merrill, assistant professor of marketing at Indiana University, explains the young single adult propensity for buying: "Everyone, to an extent, expresses their lifestyle through purchases. But for singles, those outward-appearing things let everyone know where they stand—like a badge."[1] The cloth-ing they wear matters, even the choice for Saturday shopping and lunch. I was going to say "a casual Saturday," but there was little casual about what we saw that day.

North Clark Street isn't far from Fullerton Parkway and its luxurious row houses, but for most of these young people, it is very far. Yet, maybe someday, if they remain serious in their pursuit of the good life, they can make that move to affluence in reward for their diligence.

Yet, in all their serious pursuit of life, it seems that some-thing is missing. In becoming so self-sufficient, in striking out on their own, without need of help from their parents' generation, they look to be marooned with their own wisdom. They are customers for expensive matching by people who have no personal interest in them, who have no stake in the outcome of the marriage that may result.

The amazing financial successes of so many of today's young people may have given them the impression that they do not need anything else. They can figure out their own lives. They are on the fast track. They sound good and look good. They are educated and clever and cool. What they so easily forget is that they are no more wise than their years. Looking and sounding good does not give understanding about life and work and people and the future.

As they watch for the magnificent stranger in the produce section of the groceries that have singles' nights, or along Chicago's Magnificent Mile, in one of the many thousands of classes offered as a cover for meeting people, or maybe on Rush Street on Saturday night, they seem to forget about anything except finding the person who matches their style. Who will produce in reliable fashion.

Recent statistics have not helped the feeling of panic so many of them feel, especially the women, for there are many more eligible women than men. The imbalance is particularly hard for the woman who has educated herself far above most of the men she meets, the woman who has a fine career, who wants it all—in sequence—and who now realizes that she may not get it all. Even if she does find the man, her biological time clock may have run out. He may already have all the children he wants from another marriage.

What Do They Want?
A few weeks after I was on North Clark Street, I talked with Laura, a single woman of twenty-six. She hopes that she will marry, and yet is beginning to wonder. She hears the statistics of her chances, but chooses to discount them.

Laura and I had breakfast together one Saturday to talk about her life. She said she and other women her age find it difficult to be just friends with men, because there is always the undertone, the question beneath the surface, "Will this be something more?"

She said that her friends say they are willing to wait for marriage, but that in reality they are discontented with their busy, sometimes hectic lives. They claim they want careers, but most of those speaking this way have no man available they could marry. I asked Laura if she thought they would marry soon, if they could. She said yes.

When Laura goes back to the church where she grew up, some of the older people express concern for her, asking if she has a boyfriend yet. She feels the pain of being alone. Her job as a teacher of young children has cut her off from very much adult contact in her work.

She talked about the difficulty of finding a Christian man and said that some of her friends are now dating non-Christians. They have become very disillusioned by some of the so-called Christians they dated who wanted to take advantage of them. They are finding that some of the non-Christian men they date treat them with more respect and have higher moral standards than those they met in church.

I talked with Vanessa, who is thirty-two. She has lived through a few more years of being alone than Laura and has seen more of her friends married than Laura has. When we talked, Vanessa was planning yet again to be a bridesmaid.

In the place where she works, there are some single men, and she is friends with several of them. However, she can't seem to manage this with any degree of privacy, since there are always people who feel obligated to comment on any man they see her going out to lunch with.

I was at Meg's house one day when Joan came over. She wasn't looking her cheerful self, and soon her eyes filled with tears as she told us about the upcoming wedding of her youngest brother. Joan is from a large family, and this was the last of her brothers and sisters to be married.

She said, "I guess it is just as well I am facing into this now. Maybe I'll get over it before the wedding. But I'm not taking this very well."

What she was facing was the fact that she would now be the only one of her family to be alone. At age forty, she had no prospects. True, she had an interesting job and many friends. But all of her family lived many hours away, and she had no one especially for her on a day-to-day basis.

I had lunch one day with Eileen, a young-looking woman of fifty-five who has never married. She was an only child, and has made her home all these years with her widowed mother. This arrangement has been happy for both of them.

As I asked her how she felt about never having married, she told me in some detail about two boyfriends of college days. And then she concluded by saying, "I could have been married." After a pause, she laughed and said, "Somehow it mattered that you know that."

Her concern now is about what she will do when her mother dies. She thinks about her need for security, for someone to care about her. She is at peace about her marital status, and she is a long way from Laura and Vanessa, who still have high hopes of being married.

Loneliness

According to an article in the Chicago *Tribune*, it is not true that all young women have the same desire to marry. "Many women who won't marry no doubt don't want to. Some women are unwilling to make the sacrifices that men would demand of them in marriage. Today's woman has less incentive to marry than women in the past: she does not require marriage for sustenance or for sex."[2]

Because it is more acceptable for a woman to be single today, career women don't find that they are cast as old maids, as they might have been a generation ago. But even with the degree of satisfaction they find in their work and friendships, most of them still feel unrest inside. Much of this stems from loneliness.

Loneliness can invade the spirit as surreptitiously as a disease enters the bloodstream. This malignancy thrives inside you, but it saps your energy and leaves you crippled with fear. The fear of becoming a fringe person instead of one of the group. The fear of taking the risk of giving yourself to others. Above all, the fear that the real you does not matter to anyone. . . .

Often loneliness is a jumble of feelings. It is the feeling that you matter to people only for what you can *do*, not for who you *are*. For some, it goes deeper than that: it is the anxiety that you do not matter at all. If you died tomorrow, no one would even notice, let alone care. You feel alienated, cut off by others. You think that no one is even aware of your heart hunger, your need for care, love, and support. . . .

Most of us work hard at papering over the cracks caused by loneliness. We overwork to beguile the world and ourselves into believing that all is well. And the inner bleep of loneliness refuses to be silenced. It brings us face to face with reality: not the personal success story we project to the world, but the true situation—our inner poverty.[3]

What I have just quoted is part of an article by Joyce Huggett, a counselor at St. Nicholas Church, Nottingham, England. She describes well what so many young women of today are feeling—a loneliness that contributes to a high level of anxiety. Or is it that the anxiety produces the feelings of aloneness? For there is a high degree of anxiety among single people, and especially among young women. Anxiety can be measured by the distance between expectation and fulfillment, and these women are caught in a place which makes judging that distance impossible. They don't know if fulfillment is in never-never land, or if it is just around the corner.

Years ago, when I lived in Alaska, I became aware of the depressive cabin fever so prevalent just before spring break-up. As the long winter was about to end, the loneliness and anxiety were the worst. Each year, a few people could not wait three or four more weeks, and committed suicide.

Young single women aren't dealing with a fairly predictable calendar year. They don't know if it is March or November when it comes to their anxiety and loneliness, and they find themselves in a mixed mind-set. Never do they want to lose their very normal desires for husband and children and home. Never do they want to lessen a sense of their own sexuality and of their distinctiveness as women. Never do they want to stop relating to people as women, with all that this means. And yet, they have found it safer in some situations to adopt attitudes and behaviors that have been traditionally thought of as masculine. To become more impersonal, more aggressive, and let the chips fall where they may.

They might not like themselves this way, but they don't know how else to live in their world. These young women have been raised on mixed messages, on the hope that if they just wait, a good husband will come along and give them a traditional home. But, on the other hand, on the belief that they can have it all, and that the world is their oyster.

And so, many of them alternate between being aggressive and being passive. And somewhere between the two is a reserve of anger, and a feeling of having been betrayed. Most of them cannot see life as their mothers did. Even their mothers don't see life the way they used to. Life as the feminists described it doesn't exist, and the Betty Friedans and Eleanor Smeals are now saying life isn't what they promised.

How do young women today cope with their worlds? While it is impossible to generalize about individuals, there are some characteristics of this generation that stand out.

● Some compartmentalize their lives into neat categories and do whatever seems appropriate in each place. This does appear to work for a while, for it solves the problem of dragging one world and its assumptions into another. But it doesn't work for long. For you can stretch yourself only so far before you feel stressed like a rubberband about to break.

● Some develop a carton complex, a new label for behavior that has been around a long time. The Chicago *Tribune* featured a story about Donna, a single woman with a carton complex. Donna lives in the Old Town neighborhood of Chicago and has just signed another lease on her apartment.

There's no reason to believe she'll be moving out soon. No job transfer looming. No windfall on the way for a down payment on a house. But despite the fact that Donna's immediate future seems to be right there in that Old Town one-bedroom, the corner of the dining room is piled with boxes. Cartons filled with books, with Pyrex, with things she doesn't need right away but figures she will someday. . . . She believes that sooner or later a man will enter her life and take her away from her Old Town apartment. He will take her to the North Shore or the North Side. They will set up a home together. That will be her *real* home. They will use the Pyrex together.[4]

● Some women who have achieved career success and are approaching middle age have come to terms, more or less, with their present status. Part of this is a result of watching the marriages of their friends and relatives and knowing that they are better off single than some of their friends are married. One woman said, "The difference between being unhappily single and unhappily married is that, in the first case, one phone call can turn it around. The other takes a lot more work. I enjoy having control over my environment."⁵ A particular problem for such women is that they are the cream of the crop, while never-married men their age are generally at the other end of the reckoning, unless, of course, they have stayed single for reasons of religious service.

● Some women seek to resolve their loneliness by cohabitation. Many young people believe they no longer need marriage for sexual activity. Secular magazines are flooded with references to people cohabiting, daily or now and then, with one friend or a succession of people. The woman who thinks she can be single, have career success, and also be sexually active—until she decides she wants to marry—may believe she has it all. From another point of view, she is kidding herself. She wants financial aloneness but physical pairing. She wants to spread herself as far as she wishes, a bit here, a bit there, until the day when she tries to bring herself together to decide something about a unified life.

A woman who is single but sexually active is not authentic. She is trying to live two or more lives at once. Because of her desire for money, career achievement, maybe because of fear of commitment, an inability to tolerate imperfection in a mate, or an unwillingness to spend time on who she is as a person, she avoids authentic aloneness. For a while she may think that she has a reasonable facsimile of marriage, only to find out that cohabitation wasn't anything at all like marriage.

● A 1986 article in *Psychology Today* is about the children of the 1960s who are

copping out on adulthood. They are refusing to take on the responsibilities and make the commitments necessary to become mature, functional adults with a stake in society. . . . Perhaps the reason the young adults do not welcome initiation into adulthood is not so much a reluctance to leave their childhood but rather a search for the carefree childhood they never had.⁶

34

Where Is Happiness?

On the morning Laura and I had a late breakfast together, I was amazed at my own emotional reaction to her, because it was so different from my response to talking with older women about the same subject. I felt nearly in awe of Laura's fragile and lovely desire for marriage and home, and didn't want to say anything that would show less than profound respect and regard for her desires.

At the same time, when I sensed the contradiction between what is and what she wants, I did wonder how she was going to deal with the frustrations of hoping for and not having. And so I asked her a question that came out something like, "If you knew that you would never marry, what course would you follow in your personal growth, in career development, in your personal life?"

I feel that this is the question every young woman should try to answer, even if she thinks she is well on her way to the altar. To deal with the question is to acknowledge that she has an identity and a definition other than as a potential wife. It is to take seriously her own existence as a responsible adult. It is to recognize that God relates to women directly, not only through men. While these items for recognition are obvious on an intellectual level, they are not all that obvious when we are struggling with our emotions.

One reason it is important to decide where you are going and how is that your mind can accommodate only so many things at once. If you are concentrating on goals and growth and relationships, you won't have as much time to dwell on what you don't have. Also, when you are confident that you are going someplace, you feel a sense of purpose and are less likely to enter new situations and meet new people with the raw edge of hope that "maybe this will be the day, this will be the person." Such a poignant anxiety communicates itself, whether you want it to or not.

A woman who is forever waiting comes across as dependent. This may have been attractive in Jane Austen's day, but it is far less so today. We live in a fast-paced information society that assumes we have access to the information we need to make things happen *for* us. There is little patience with people who wait for things to happen *to* them.

A complication for many young women is that they were raised to think that they were supposed to wait for Prince Charming to come and kiss them into real life. Then they, like Pinocchio, would become real people. They, like Cinderella, perhaps misunderstood, unappreciated, wouldn't have to fear, because the prince would come along eventually and be an exact match. Yet, even the fairy godmother couldn't keep Cinderella's coach from turning into a pumpkin. Even the forces of good couldn't keep the princess from falling into a deep sleep, or the prince from becoming a frog.

Somehow we have based our theology on Aladdin's magic lamp more than on the Scriptures, on the flying carpet more than on God's glass of reflection. This leads us to expect and ask all manner of things that are contradictory to one another and out of sync with life. When our prayers are not answered, we know someone is to blame, probably God. Or maybe ourselves, because we didn't pray right, or didn't have enough faith, or weren't good enough or attractive enough, or didn't have the right parents, and so on.

One indicator of maturity is the ability to face reality. Since there are more women than men of marriageable age, we must assume that many women are not going to find husbands. Some of the best women, in fact. I hope that as you examine the realities of your life, you will also examine God's ways with people, as shown to us in the Bible, and come to understand those principles which apply to life today.

If ever there was a woman who had reason to be unhappy and bitter about what had been handed to her by life, it was Helen Keller. Yet somehow—through the love of family and by the grace of God—she came to peace and to fullness of life. She expressed her thoughts in these moving words:

Happiness cannot come from without.
It must come from within.
It is not what we see and touch
Or that which others do for us
which makes us happy;
it is that which we think and feel and do,
first for the other fellow
and then for ourselves.'

36

4

"JESUS, YOU'RE LATE!"

May the burden of the dark cloud
when it appears on the mountain peak
never fall upon your shoulders,
nor its malevolent hail
impair your wings.

Esteban Manuel de Villegas 1589–1669

I am waiting for a dawn that never comes. . . .
I am hedged in by God on every side. . . .
I have no peace of mind nor quiet. . . .
Though I am right, I get no answer. . . .
I tremble in every nerve. . . .
God Himself has put me in the wrong. . . .
God has hedged in my road. . . .
God has pulled up my tent-rope. . . .
My thoughts are resentful and I would state my case!

Job

While crisis and loss can come to women of any age, they seem
to concentrate in a special way on women in their middle
years . . . women confronting physical and emotional changes
within themselves, lamenting the loss of youth and its possibilities, but still trying to fulfill some of their dreams . . . women
watching elderly parents wane in strength and eventually pass

on, often after long care.

Women who have been married but are suddenly single now face a totally new way of life. Because of being divorced or widowed, they live in reduced circumstances economically and in a narrowed world socially, and at times feel as if they are watching the world go by.

One such woman, divorced after a long marriage, said to me, "Life goes on—that's all. It just goes on, nothing more." Many of these middle-life women are mothers who are forced to deal with or helplessly watch some very difficult problems in the lives of their teenage and adult children.

So many kinds of losses can come to a woman of middle years—the loss of a job, the loss of being needed, the loss of friends by death or a move, the loss of beauty, of health, of confidence. The years that, by rights, should boast a golden sheen are tarnished by wear.

Even when there is no crisis point, we can still at times experience a profound sense of loss which is hard to explain, because it is not connected with something that was and is no longer. Rather, it feels more like the absence of something that should have been and never was. A love we craved that never came to us. A favor we wanted to enjoy but never experienced. A promise that was made but never kept. A sense of alienation, cutting us off from the flow of life. An emptiness that leaves us unable to meet the challenges of normal living.

All loss is a kind of death. Yet, only as we learn to live with death can we truly relish life.

Two women named Mary and one named Martha had to look at the death of loved ones. In their stories we can see ourselves as we deal with the losses in our lives.

Mother

There is something unnatural about watching a child die. The child should eventually bury the parent, not the parent the child. There is no more poignant picture of a mother suffering for a dying child than of Mary standing beneath the cross on which her Son was nailed. For what crime? For being what she bore Him to become. For being what was promised.

In his *Messiah*, George Frederic Handel draws words from Lamentations to ask, "Behold and see if there be any sorrow like unto His sorrow." And yet, on a strictly human level, there must have been no greater sorrow than Mary's. For in those hours, her mother heart saw the baby in her arms, the toddler, the little boy learning of the world, the boy-man of twelve whose voice was changing at the very time He sat with the elders in the temple.

Her little boy was spread out on that cross, spikes splitting the hands she had cared for, the fingernails she had trimmed. The mouth that had taken her milk was now swollen from thirst and being given vinegar to drink. Her boy—the outrage. And yet, even in those hours of suffering, Mary was sharing in the ultimate blessing that would come to the world. Whatever battles were fought and whatever strongholds were brought down would bless her. The sufferings of her Son would liberate her along with so many others.

During His pain, her Son thought of her. He saw her with His young friend, John, and spoke to them both, giving them into each other's care in a new relationship of love.

Christ understood the reason for what He was enduring, and its result. We of the short sight and clouded understanding know so little of reasons, results, or remedies. Yet in a small but significant way, the physical and emotional sufferings of our own children can be redemptive to us, as well as to them.

Mothers alone often watch their children go through years of pain that they cannot take away, problems they can do little to solve, questions they can't adequately answer. Sometimes, in the middle of the confusion and hurt, our children think of us, of our pain, our need to grow and become more than we are, and they urge us along, so that their pain becomes redemptive for us as well.

If this is your story, learn to listen to what your children are trying to convey to you. Learn to look beyond their anger, especially if some of it is directed at you. For beyond the frustration, you may hear some concern for you. They may be expressing a legitimate criticism about you, may be telling you something you truly need to change about yourself. They may want you to live more fully, to express who you are on a higher level. When this desire comes out joined to frustration, it is hard to hear the redemptive part of it. But as you listen and look more closely at a child who feels forsaken, who thirsts and is given vinegar, who loves and is reviled by someone who should be close to him, and when you are in despair along with your child, you may hear, "Woman, there is a new way. There is another opportunity. There is a different place for you. A new relationship. Reach out to someone else. Receive care from another. Don't stop loving. Know that life will change, but that love will go on."

I had such an experience with my son. Once I got past the confusion of what he was saying to me, once I began to understand the love, I realized that words which sounded critical were really a challenge to further become and grow.

What confused me at first was that he was speaking from the context of his own unmet needs, and I felt some guilt about those. When I finally understood, I felt deep thanks for a son who could build a bridge over his own losses and say, "Mom, you can come across. I'll help you."

I had tried to bridge so much for him, and yet this time, he built a bridge with my name on it, and was trying to lead me in an enlarged way. It mattered very much to him that I became all I could be. His concern was special to me because I hadn't expected it.

And yet . . . the suggestion that we should change . . . coming from our own children? The idea that we are not fully okay? That we are not enough as we are? Our own children, for whom we have sacrificed, saying this to us?

Yes, our children, who also have lost and suffered, whose hurts are as legitimate as ours, and who can still think of someone else.

Sisters

Jesus knew that Lazarus was going to die, and He purposely stayed away. When He and the disciples finally arrived in Bethany, Lazarus had already been buried for four days, and his sisters and friends were grieving. Martha met Him first. Her words, "Lord, if You had been here, my brother would not have died. And I know that even now whatever You ask of God, He will grant You."

Jesus replied, "Your brother will rise again." She answered, "I know that he will rise again in the resurrection on the last day."

40

Then Jesus said to her, "I am the Resurrection and the Life; the believer in Me will live even when he dies, and everyone who lives and believes in Me shall never, never die. Do you believe this?"

Martha said, "Yes, Lord. I have faith that Thou art the Christ, the Son of God, who was to come into the world."

Then Martha went off to tell Mary that Jesus had come. Mary met Him with exactly the same words, "Lord, had You been here, my brother would not have died." But she ended it there.[1]

In the interchange with Martha, we can feel her expectancy that Jesus could raise her brother from the dead, if He chose. But He ignored that hope for the moment and pressed on to the matter of belief, telling her who He was in unforgettable terms. His question to Martha, "Do you believe?" is the question for us when we too face the loss of someone we love. It is not whether we believe in a possible instant resurrection, but whether we believe in Christ as the Resurrection and the Life, as the One who ultimately conquers all sin and death and sickness.

When your parent dies, or your sister or brother, or a loved grandparent or a child, do you believe in Jesus as the Resurrection and the Life for that one you now miss so severely? Do you believe in Jesus as your Resurrection and Life? His question cuts through our accusations of what He did not do and our hopes of what He might do. It puts us on the line—do you believe?

As I brought Mary and Martha closer to our own day, I heard more clearly what they were saying to Jesus. "You're late. You're too late."

From our perspective, Jesus is often late. He is too late to keep us from being the way we are. By the time He arrives, bad things have happened to us, or we have messed up in some way. We have done too much of one thing, not enough of another, have gone to excess, have followed the eccentricities of our minds, the waywardness of our inclinations, the lethargy of our wills, the weakness of our constitutions, and by the time we are aware of His presence, we haven't much in our hands to recommend us.

He comes too late to prevent the wrongs people do to us,

REFLECTIONS FOR WOMEN ALONE

which we in turn pass on to others. He comes too late to stop war and disease and sin, and His tardiness angers us, so that instead of admitting what we are—helpless, lost, losing, crisis-prone, weak, and at best not wise enough, not loving enough—we are likely to excuse ourselves as victims in His absence, and not truly responsible.

Benevolent and easy-going Father,
We have occasionally been guilty of errors of judgment.
We have lived under the deprivations of heredity
    and the disadvantages of environment.
We have sometimes failed to act in accordance with com-
    mon sense.
We have done the best we could in the circumstances;
And have been careful not to ignore the common standards
    of decency;
And we are glad to think that we are fairly normal.

Do Thou, O Lord, deal lightly with our infrequent lapses.
Be Thy own sweet Self with those who admit they are not
    perfect;
According to the unlimited tolerance which we have a right
    to expect from Thee.
And grant us an indulgent Parent that we may hereafter
    continue to live a harmless and happy life and keep our
    self-respect.[2]

Because of the kind of world we live in, Jesus will always seem to be late, too late to prevent wrong and ill. Too late to stop us from our natural inclinations. Too late to shelter us from the normal cycles of illness and death. God has given free choice, and sin and weakness are the results.

But Jesus is often late deliberately, so that we might grow and become and be refined and develop into strong people of God. As Peter wrote to the scattered Christians of his day, he admitted that Jesus would delay for a time, "but after you have suffered for a while . . . He will strengthen, establish you."

We don't like that. We want life on our terms, as a reward for believing, but confrontation with a crisis does put us to the wall where we have to be more honest in our praying. More honest with ourselves. Trouble is no time for waffling, for making excuses. It is a time to see ourselves as we are, to look in the glass of God's mirror, and to ask for clear sight. It is a time to pray the confession rightly:

Almighty and most merciful Father,
We have erred, and strayed from Thy ways like lost sheep.
We have followed too much the devices and desires of our
  own hearts.
We have offended against Thy holy laws.
We have left undone those things which we ought to have
  done.
And we have done those things which we ought not to
  have done;
And there is no health in us.

But Thou, O Lord, have mercy upon us, miserable
  offenders.
Spare Thou those, O God, who confess their faults.
Restore Thou those who are penitent;
According to Thy promises declared unto mankind in
  Christ Jesus our Lord.
And grant, O most merciful Father, for His sake,
That we may hereafter live a godly, righteous and sober
  life,
To the glory of Thy holy name.
Amen.[3]

5

STRANGER IN MY MIRROR

What dignity it gives an old lady,
that balance at the banker's!
How tenderly we look at her faults,
if she is a relative (and may every
reader have a score of such),
what a kind, good-natured old creature we find her . . .
how, when she comes to pay us a visit,
we generally find an opportunity to let
our friends know her station in the world . . .

Ah, gracious powers!
I wish you would send me an old aunt—a maiden aunt—
an aunt with a lozenge on her carriage
and a front of light coffee-colored hair—
how my children should work workbags for her,
and my Julia and I would make her comfortable!
Sweet—sweet vision! Foolish—foolish dream!

William Makepeace Thackeray

In America, the fear of dying early has been
replaced by the fear of living too long.

A life insurance ad

It was on a day when I stayed home from work, not seriously ill,
but not feeling very well either. My mail came early that

44

afternoon, bringing letters from two organizations I had not heard from before.

The American Association of Retired Persons wanted me to join their ranks, or at least take their magazine, so that my life would be enriched.

The second letter was even more cheerful. If I would subscribe to the American Plan, I would receive a Memorial Guide in which I could note my wishes for my final disposal. The company would make sure that a photocopy of my wishes was sent to the funeral director of my choice.

After reading my mail, I wondered if these items might have seemed more humorous had I been married. For the rather stark fact is that I do face the years ahead alone. And yet the same reality is ahead of most women. Even if they have married, the majority will spend their later years alone.

I hope I am far from my last years, and I felt slightly annoyed at receiving mail like those two pieces just yet. But the need to plan for old age no one can deny. I have watched my mother and others her age do this, with varying results. Their choices reflect their emotions as much as they do their purses, or more.

There was another piece of mail that day, from a book club, advertising Dr. Seuss's new book, *You're Only Old Once.* Instead of sending in the order, I called a discount bookstore. I may get old only once, but I am part Scot always, and I don't like to pay full price for anything. A few days later, I picked up the book and gave it to my mother, who three years ago bought an apartment in a retirement home. After several weeks, I asked her if she had shown the book to any of her friends. She hadn't—she didn't think they would find it funny. Maybe they are too young yet!

There is something about being old that is hard on the person inside. When my daughter was a social worker in a retirement home, one of the women said to her, "I feel so young and then I look in my mirror and see a stranger looking back at me." If this woman had had a husband who looked at her through ever-young eyes, or someone she had known as a young woman, she might not have been so jarred by what she saw in the mirror. But being alone—as most of the people in that home were— helped to set that reflection in a finality that made a deep impression on her. What she was seeing was the way it was.

45

To be old can be difficult, but to be old and alone is worse yet. To be old and alone and afraid of what might happen to you is the worst. What happens is never as bad as the anticipation, because then you know. Then you are not dealing with the "what ifs" any longer.

In his book *Lake Wobegon Days*, Garrison Keillor records an exchange between two older women in his town, Charlotte and Ella. Charlotte is at Ella's house.

> One night she sat at Ella's kitchen table, cutting up cucumbers, and suddenly dropped the knife and said, "I don't know what I'm going to do when you're gone," and cried bitterly, and Ella tried to comfort her.
>
> "Don't worry, I feel just fine," she said. Ella doesn't think about death much herself. Not as much as she did thirty years ago. She thinks about visitors. Loneliness is too dramatic. It makes troubles seem tragic, and hers are quite ordinary old-lady troubles, she thinks, and would seem more ordinary if she had some ordinary visitors. Not like Charlotte. Charlotte is an event.[1]

What do older women alone need? Especially those who are in the second phase of older, those well into their seventies? They need just the same things that younger women need, but in slightly different ways. They need people to care about them, but with an added element of security. They need a place where they belong, and where they can feel assured of staying. They need something significant to do, but geared to their interests and energy level.

In the early years of retirement, most people can function very well in the normal community. If they are well and have energy and imagination they can fill their calendars with worthwhile and enjoyable things to do, often to such an extent that they have close to a work schedule again.

I think of Bernice, a widow of three years who volunteers her time in the foundation office of the company where I work. She won't accept any money for her work and puts in close to the number of hours of paid employees.

I think of Henrietta, an older widow of many years, who has particular concern for the sanctity-of-life issue. Her contribution to saving unborn lives is to serve as a foster mother to unwed mothers in the several months before they give birth. She does this as a ministry to the Lord.

I think of older people in my church who give time to Christian organizations in the Wheaton area. I don't know how these agencies would continue to function without such help.

My mother was in Florida when my father died, three years after their move to Seminole. She stayed there for twelve years of active involvement in her church, hosting a Bible study in her home, serving as chairman of the Women's Missionary Society and as president of her Sunday School class. She traveled some, had many friends she saw regularly, made her way north to visit with family a few times a year, and kept a pace that I could almost match.

But then something happened, and not all at once. She watched a few of her friends begin to decline in their ability to manage their own lives. They couldn't drive anymore. Just caring for themselves became a full-time chore. They no longer were able to entertain. They developed physical problems and had a hard time shopping, cooking, even deciding about everyday things. Mother and a few others tried to take care of these women. She saw what happened as her friends were now too old or sick to make good decisions for themselves and yet were resisting the suggestions of their children or other relatives. There had to be a change in their way of life, and this was so hard for them to think about.

After watching all of this, Mother made a decision that had been in the back of her mind for some years, since 1978 when she had put a small amount of money in a retirement home of the Evangelical Free Church, just in case she would want to live there someday. Right after Christmas of 1984, she moved to Rockford, Illinois, and today is living in a lovely apartment, has many friends, is involved in her new church, travels, attends concert series, comes often to visit the family, makes items for the sales the home has, plays the organ for their daily chapel services, and more. The quality of life has not changed as much as the security level has. Now I no longer hear sentences that begin with, "What if . . . " The what ifs are all answered. There really isn't anything that could happen that would not be taken care of.

In the past, most retirement homes were built in California,

Arizona, or Florida. It is most encouraging now to see more of them being constructed nearer the places people have lived, nearer to friends and family. Now older people don't have to choose between independence and family.

The prospect of moving in with children and grandchildren is not much more attractive to the average older person than it is to the children. Our way of life and type of housing just don't make such arrangements easy. And most people don't have enough money to comfortably be able to plan for separate but close housing, and also to cover outrageous medical costs that lie in front of them as real possibilities.

With my daughter working in one retirement home and my mother living in another, I found myself learning from both sides about a way of life that has many advantages. The people are with others of their age. Their basic needs are cared for, they have financial stability, their medical needs will be taken care of, and they can maintain their independence.

We Need Older Relatives
In the year of writing this book, I became a grandmother. Twelve days after my granddaughter was born, my mother came to town, and we took our first four-generation picture, Marion, Carole, Catherine, and new Lindsey Anne. I was reminded of how fortunate I feel to live close to my children, and to see them and now Lindsey on a regular basis. And I was reminded of what Page Smith had said about grandmothers in his book, *Daughters of the Promised Land*.

One of the particular losses women have experienced in America is in their function as grandmother. As late as the nineteenth century the grandmother was deemed to have an essential role in the nurture of her grandchildren; she was a living repository of traditional wisdom, of painfully accumulated experience that touched every aspect of domestic existence. Most important, the grandmother mediated the child to its parents. The relation of parents to child is an intense and often emotion-charged one; the grandmother was an intermediary. She had *time;* time that a busy mother or harassed father did not have, and her time spans coincided with the child's. Her stories of the child's parents' childhood

48

made the parents understandably human for the child, gave them a stronger reality as people whose lives had a depth and texture not readily revealed in day-to-day relations within the family. It is always an enthralling experience for a child to discover the childhood of its parents.

Many of the tensions of the modern "nuclear" family are the consequence of the absence of this traditional mediator, the grandmother. . . . America, I believe, needs grandmothers. . . We need them for our souls' sakes and for theirs.[2]

What can be said about the grandmother role can also be said about the aunt, the great-aunt, the older cousin, the godmother, any older woman who functions like family for younger people. I have seen situations in which younger families and older people have adopted one another as substitute family, and this can be a rich experience. Relatives in Portland, Oregon live next to a single woman of ninety-two who is in good health and lives alone in her own home. My relatives help her with yard work and screens and painting trim and rides to town. But they do more—they include her in birthday celebrations and always spend Christmas Eve with her. The giving is not all on one side, of course; they feel enriched from their friendship with her, and are glad that their children have had such close contact with an older woman, since their grandparents live far away.

Older Women at Church
As people are living longer and there are more and more of them, they become a force to be reckoned with. Most churches have some sort of grouping for the elderly, if only a special Sunday School class, and many churches offer educational and social opportunities. But too often, the church has adopted the attitude of the economic sphere which assumes that when earning power has decreased, everything else is nearly gone too. The phasing out we see in the work scene is not far from what happens in many churches, and this should not be. We should make opportunity for the older people to teach the younger, and for intergenerational activities, particularly between the grandchild and grandparent age span. Older people should not be overlooked as teachers and board members. They should not

feel pushed to one side by the sheer energy level of a youth-oriented society.

In our churches we can't afford to lose a whole segment of our membership by neglect. Nor can we afford, before the Lord, to let these people feel that God and His people have forgotten them, or that they just don't matter now that their incomes are less than they were ten or twenty years ago.

They should not be ignored when it comes to parties and entertainment. Some of the most relaxed and funny people around are those who have lived a long time. Two years ago, at a writer's conference I attended in Washington State, five of the conferees were over eighty. This was a surprising proportion of the total, and we wondered how they would get along. We didn't have to worry. They were the stars of the week as they entertained us all with humor that moved from wry to outrageous to self-serving so fast that we could hardly keep up with it. They were at their best in front of the whole group, with a relaxation that most younger people find hard to match. There was nothing left to prove. Nothing to earn. No wars to win. No life philosophy to hammer out. No children to raise. Nothing left but to be and to enjoy and to love and to do good for others.

In the Old Testament, there are four places that speak of someone dying in a good old age. Psalm 92:14-15 shows us a lovely picture of the older righteous person, "vigorous in old age like trees full of sap, luxuriant, wide-spreading, eager to declare that the Lord is just, the Lord my rock, in whom there is no unrighteousness."[3] In Isaiah 46 we hear the Lord speaking to the house of Jacob, "A load on Me from your birth, carried by Me from the womb: till you grow old, I am He, and when white hairs come, I will carry you still; I have made you and I will bear the burden, I will carry you and bring you to safety."[4]

6

THE MIRROR OF FRIENDSHIP

May heaven protect us, cher monsieur,
from being set on a pedestal by our friends!

Albert Camus

All relationship must be reciprocal . . .
I am being killed when there is no one to receive
my thoughts, my feelings, my innermost self.

Elizabeth O'Connor

Friendship is an important subject today, partly because its antithesis, loneliness and isolation, is so common. Most of us do not live in a town that has known our parents and grandparents. We no longer have extended family nearby. We work hard for a sense of community, a little here and a little there, and the prospect of having to go out yet another night to find a missing piece for the friendship puzzle can in itself be tiring. This is why there is greater emphasis on digging in to stay with friends we have already made.

In an article in the Chicago *Tribune*, Lisa Anderson wrote:

It's the hottest topic on prime-time TV and an increasing theme of chart-hopping records. Not only is it big at the box office but it's playing a dramatically different and more important role in our lives than ever before. It's friendship—and it may well wind up as the sociological signature of the

80s. . . . However, it is friendship in a significantly new role. In earlier times friends ran a far second to an extended family as the major source of social and emotional support in a person's life. But for many people nowadays, friendship is not an option, it is a necessity. . . .

Never before have we expected or demanded so much from ourselves and our partners and never before in history have we so lacked the kind of kinship support that families and marriages always had in the past.'

The Hidden Agenda

As I was preparing for writing this book, I had lunch with Barbara, who is almost old enough to be my mother. She is still working full-time and living at an energetic pace. When I asked her about friendships for women alone, she said, "It doesn't work to come to a potential friendship with a hidden agenda. If we want or need something specific from the other person or from the friendship, the relationship just isn't going to work."

If Barbara is right, and I suspect she is, that puts many women alone in quite a bind, for they do have needs, and they do carry expectations that their friends will meet those needs. They feel the stress of continually reaching out—alone—to new people, new groups, people they hope will be friends, and at the same time wondering if it is going to be worth the effort.

The hidden agenda goes both ways, hoping people will like us and want to be our friends, but also needing to protect ourselves against overinvolvement and pursuit of the unrealistic. Sometimes the need for being with people seems almost a barter—"If I go, will they make it worth my while?" Not a good beginning, certainly, but one that happens all too often.

At times the whole friendship scene can look and sound like "Let's Make a Deal." A trade-off. The religious vendors of good feelings tell us that if we are friends to ourselves, we will be happy and successful. If we are friends with God, He will favor and prosper us. If we can find useful friends out there, they will help us and make us look good. Almost without thinking about it, those of us who deplore such bargaining can find ourselves responding on a pragmatic level. We want to matter. We need to be significant, and we are willing to go to considerable lengths to meet this need.

As I travel for my work, I run into people from other parts of the country who come together at conventions and meetings. And I am often amused to hear someone introducing casual acquaintances as "good friends," and even more startled when I hear myself referred to as a close friend of someone I have seen all of three times and probably will never be close to.

What I am seeing is networking, and often with very nice people, many of whom would be fine "good friends" if we were ever together long enough to learn about one another, to begin to understand what life is like for the other. These acquaintances play their part in my life and I do enjoy seeing them. They give life and sparkle to what could be a lonely time away from home, and I try to give to them in ways that will meet whatever surface needs we are comfortable with sharing.

I would never downplay the people in my network, for already some of them have become friends. We have moved to the level of spending enough time now and then to begin to appreciate what is happening in our lives when there is no convention, no travel, no glamour, no audience.

Friendship and Nurture

Some of us are slow to learn the meanings of friendship. While this slowness can come from various causes, many of us share in one reason for the tardiness—we are not sufficiently good friends to ourselves. When we ignore or denigrate our own value, we find it hard to believe that others place high value on us. We also fail to appreciate what God feels for us.

I ran into this at a meeting I was attending for my work. A session had just ended when the person next to me suddenly said, "I don't know how to be a part of a nurturing relationship," and then elaborated on the feeling of inability. I was stunned, since this isn't the sort of remark you hear every day, and particularly in a space of time usually given to small talk. And above all, from a person who exuded such confidence.

Many of us are short on nurture. We didn't get enough when we were young. We didn't see other people giving it sufficiently to even know how to apply nurture to those around us. Or we were taught that girls and women are the nurturers, the givers, and should not expect to receive.

In 1985, I came across an insightful book about nurture, *What*

Do Women Want? by Luise Eichenbaum and Susie Orbach. In part, the book is a response to *The Cinderella Complex*, which portrayed women as childlike figures who want to be dependents. Eichenbaum and Orbach claim that the author of *The Cinderella Complex* has drawn erroneous conclusions from her research. Their studies and clinical counseling have demonstrated to them that it is generally a lack of nurture, and not a desire to be dependent, that has held women back from venturing out into the world with the same eagerness so many men show.

Women are indeed fearful of independence and success. But this is not because they have been raised to depend on others. It is precisely for the opposite reason: women are raised to be depended upon; to place their emotional needs second to those of others. . . .

In our society too few people receive the kind of nurturance that allows them to anticipate relationships with joy Our early relationships can be fraught with disappointment and misunderstanding. Many of us live with a missing piece inside, a confusion and worry; we yearn for a soul mate who will love us, understand us and help us face ourselves. Many of us have a needy part that is hidden away from the world and from ourselves. . . .

Women, who on the face of it seem to be the dependent sex, are in reality involved in a cruel and unequal bargain that diminishes both men and women. Women are reared to provide for the dependency needs of others, to respond emotionally to their children, husbands, work mates, etc. Women develop emotional antennae that alert them to the needs of others. Women help those close to them process the disagreeable emotions that come up on a day-to-day basis. . . . Women, almost instinctively, pick up on the concerns of others—including other women—and find one way or another to help the person come to terms with whatever is at hand. *What is missing in women's lives is that they have never had the consistent experience of this being done for them.*[2]

Friendships With Men

Women alone need men friends. We need men whose opinions we can ask about things that matter to us. We need to be part of mixed groups. While nonromantic friendship between men and women can be difficult to manage, it can also offer the highest of rewards. In my reading in preparation for this book, I didn't expect to come across so many women who had benefited from friendships with men. Catherine of Siena was a good friend of Raymond of Capua in the fourteenth century. Queen Margaret of Scotland, in the eleventh century, was a special friend to Lanfranc. Poet Hannah More in eighteenth-century England was good friends with John Newton, Dr. Samuel Johnson, William Wilberforce, and David Garrick. Madam Guyon found guidance and inspiration from Fénelon and Francis Lacombe. Clare founded the Poor Clares as a sister order to the Franciscans, and in close friendship, she and Francis guided the purposes of these similar orders. We think of Paula and Jerome, Marcella and Jerome, Macrina and Gregory—a brother and sister friendship—and Teresa and St. John of the Cross.

Many of these friendships were, of course, a type that is not available to most people today. But then, we don't need the same thing as they had. Our needs are in the context of our own time and place. There may be a couple or two with whom you can deepen your friendship. You might have a male relative to whom you would like to be closer. Within a work setting, good friendships often develop, offering support in one of the most challenging and stressful areas of life.

One reason we have difficulty with male-female relationships is the way we regard our sexuality. The part of us that calls for closer bonding also causes us to be afraid and pull back. The more we struggle with this, the more we tend to see our sexuality in physical and erotic terms. Yet, friendship calls on all that we are as women to meet all that men are as people, in a complementary relationship. We want to be seen as sexual beings, and yet we may define this too narrowly. The more narrow we become, the more nervous we may become, and so lessen our chances of developing good friendships with men.

Within His culture, Jesus' behavior toward women was quite shocking, as He reached out in friendship and to meet needs. One woman who had become a special friend was Mary of Bethany, and when Jesus visited the home she shared with her sister and brother, Mary would stop what she was doing to sit and talk with Jesus, and learn from Him. It seems that she came closer to understanding His innerness and His mission in life than any other of His followers.

And yet, understanding is a long distance from her display of devotion, in which she anointed Him in preparation for His death. What she wanted to do for Jesus was so far out of the ordinary that it was risky, bold, costly, and it put her in a most vulnerable position. How easy it would have been for her to imagine herself anointing Him and to pull back, to convince herself that it wouldn't be understood. That Jesus could know her heart without a public display.

The conversations between Jesus and Mary aren't recorded for us, but if they were, I think they would show that He had bared His feelings to her as much as to anyone, that He not only indicated what He had to accomplish for the redemption of the world, but also something of the cost to Himself.

Still, it was only after an experience of loss, the death of her brother, Lazarus, and his resurrection to life, that Mary brought the ointment to the house of Simon.

On a day of crisis and joy, we often see ourselves in a new way. It is as if all the lights suddenly are lit and we are found in our inadequacy, holding our wrong expectations.

I believe Mary's deed expressed not only gratitude about her brother, but something deeper that had to do with a new look at herself in relation to Christ, her limitedness in contrast to His infiniteness, her self-absorption compared with His transparency, her shortsightedness contrasted with His perspective, her needs alongside His supply. Her act was for the enlargement of her own spirit, by One who cannot stay confined to our little imaginations, who is ever holding out to us in the glass of reflection what He sees we can be.

On a day when life and death all merged in one grand display of compassion and power, Mary saw her friend Jesus as she had never before, and was impelled to move from the comfortable to the extravagant.

Jesus had spent lavishly on their friendship. Nothing she did could match the extravagance of His long reach into death to bring back her brother. For Mary, it was not a question of repayment, rather of wanting to learn how to live as He did.

Blessed Are the Personal

We all want people to be personal to us, and that very desire settles the same responsibility on us. In his excellent book, *Happy Are You Who Affirm*, Thomas A. Kane discusses seven essentials of being personal, of giving affirmation. They are trust, approval, recognition, appreciation, reconciliation, reverence, and contemplation. These involve the relationship between a person and God, as well as that between two friends.[3]

While we all value the personal touch, while we all want to be affirmed by others, we do not naturally behave this way. At work or in social situations, we all arrive with our own agendas, and we hope that what happens will help us to achieve what we want. Without deliberate thought for being personal to other people we can all too easily forget about it.

Yet, as Christians, we should not be forgetting, for we have the ultimate example of being personal in the Holy Spirit, the One who comes alongside to encourage, to teach, to comfort, to guide, to chide, to urge us on in becoming more like Jesus, who in humility and love came into our world so that we can forever be a part of His world.

In being personal to others, at work, in the church, at home, we are always reaching for what is there, just under the surface. We are not dealing with the nonexistent but the already-formed reality. When we are personal to others, we work as midwives, drawing new life into the light of day. Such work must be done with reverence and great respect, for we are dealing with the innerness of a human being who is made in the image of God.

> To love someone is to bid him to live, invite him to grow. . . . Since people don't have the courage to mature unless someone has faith in them, we have to reach those we meet at the level where they stopped developing, where they were given up as hopeless, and so withdrew into themselves and began to secrete a protective shell because they thought they were alone and no one cared.
>
> They have to feel they're loved very deeply and very boldly before they dare appear humble and kind, affectionate, sincere and vulnerable.[4]

The book *Kabloona* is the story of the year French Count Gontron de Poncius spent with the Canadian Eskimos, in

1938–1939. At Pelly Bay, he stayed for a few weeks with Father Henry, a missionary who had lived six years with the Arviligjuarmuit people. As the Count was leaving, he and Father Henry exchanged gifts. Then the priest took Gontron's hands in his and said, "Your visit has done me a great deal of good. I believe that I shall be a better man for your having been here."

Gontron said, "I have wandered pretty much everywhere; nowhere have I heard words more beautiful."[5]

Being Friends with God

Knowing ourselves as God's friends means feeling friendly toward ourselves. It means accepting God's estimate of us, past, present, and future, and working with Him as He draws those time lines ever closer together so that His long purposes for us begin to take shape.

In moments of honest introspection, when we consider our motivations and behaviors over many years, we have to wonder why God wants us as friends. We have lived through all the wanderings, the craziness we try to conceal from others, and on some days we don't even want to be friends with ourselves. Friendship with God touches all the times of our lives, as we are forgiven for things past, understood and loved and accepted as we are on any given day, and relentlessly urged on to become, to move closer to His family likeness.

God is the founder of the Becoming Business. He wants us to develop into all that He knows we can become. But there is a condition. When the tag goes on the product, somewhere along the line, it bears His name, not ours. For part of the becoming is learning to live with glory, and that is all His. That is why the Apostle Paul spoke of us as earthen vessels, not so grand or valuable in themselves, but fully adequate for containing the treasure that comes from God alone.

Why does God want us as His friends? While we know some of the reasons, many of them remain a mystery. Yet, within our unknowing, we can receive His acceptance and bask in His love and gradually open the eyes of our understanding, as we reflect as in a mirror the splendor of the Lord and are transfigured into His likeness.[6]

7

TOO MUCH EFFORT

"Mother cried silently,"
the little boy said,
as if to chide the one
he thought was causing pain.

Little could he know
how often and for what
she cried in silence,
or that anyone had heard.

CSS

Without "harmony of dispositions . . . " marriage is but a continual fornication, sealed with an oath."

John Donne

One of the most profound kinds of aloneness is that of a woman who is legally married but alone in heart and mind. Such aloneness can result from many causes, all of them bad, for they militate against what God intends marriage to be.

The married-but-single woman appears wedded. Usually she cooperates with the public appearance that all is well, yet wanting to call out, "This is no marriage—this is a farce. A sham. Help me, somebody!"

Instead, she smiles and later goes home to cry alone. She wants so much to be valued for herself and for what she does, but seldom is. She wants to be thought attractive but knows she is thought a dog. She wants to be considered competent, and cringes when someone speaks of her as a child unable to bear adult responsibility.

She needs a recognizable reflection of herself so that she can grow. But in the mirror of at least one of those close at hand, she sees herself as without value, unattractive, dumb; and try as she will, she cannot erase that reflection.

She looks in her mirror when she is alone and smiles and tries to appear her best and to print *that* image on her heart. And sometimes it almost works, until she hears a voice, "What do you know?" or, "If you don't like things exactly as they are around here, get out!" and her value is demolished for another day. She has no advocate.

No human being has the right to imprison another in fear and humiliation.

When a woman is living in an impossible situation, she should seek help. She needs to remember that she has a future. She has a past in the love of God. She has present obligations that need her energy and competence. She is not the source of universal wrong. She is not to blame for the weather, for another's aches and pains, or for car trouble.

Many women who take the blame for everything today have been doing the same thing for years. They have lived with an oppression that has worsened over time, and their submission to wrong has only compounded the problem. By giving in to oppression, they have allowed it to continue.

Such women need hope that there is something good ahead. A verse in Psalms speaks of the days when we almost cave in and quit, except for one thing—hope. "I would have despaired unless I had believed that I would see the goodness of the Lord in the land of the living."[1]

Life in a cruel environment can take the heart out of you, until you become convinced that you deserve nothing better.

While we should not decide our commitments on the basis of what we "deserve," yet deep within us we know that certain things should not happen to us or to anyone; and in that sense, we feel that we do not deserve them. We know that physical cruelty is wrong. We know that continual insult is wrong. We know that lying and infidelity are wrong.

And if they are wrong, a woman is wrong to allow them to go on unchecked, unchallenged.

Radegonde
In the first half of the sixteenth century, two girls were born in Europe who later became known for their faith and courage during disastrous marriages.

Radegonde was a daughter of a prince of Thuringia. In 1531, when she was twelve years old, the Franks invaded her country and captured her. She was educated in the court of Chlotar I, who decided that she would make an excellent queen for him. "He was the son of the Christian Queen Clotilda, but possessed none of his mother's spiritual qualities. Radegonde did not wish to marry a man of such evil character; but after being forced into the marriage, she turned to her religion for strength."[2]

In his *History of the Franks*, Gregory of Tours wrote that "Chlotar 'unjustly' killed Radegonde's brother; perhaps this was the occasion for her asking Medard, bishop of Noyon, to allow her to become a nun. Medard finally agreed, and she entered a convent; later she founded the nunnery of the Holy Cross at Poitiers."[3]

While Chlotar was very opposed to her entering the convent, "in the end he begged her forgiveness for all the sorrow he had caused her, as well as for the massacre of many of her family, the destruction of much in Thuringia that she held dear, and later the murder of her brother. Radegonde continued to pray for her husband but she did not return to him."[4]

Jane
The second girl was born in England in 1537. Her story is as much about power as about marriage. Great-granddaughter to Henry VII, Lady Jane Grey lived one hundred years before the power of the English throne was broken, in a time of intense conflict between Catholics and Protestants, as both groups fought to insure their own freedoms.

Jane grew up with socially ambitious parents in a world of ruthless and power-hungry people. A few individuals provided love and nurture for the young girl. Catherine Parr was one. Another was Miles Coverdale, one of her tutors and the chaplain for the Greys. In *Coronation of Glory*, Deborah Meroff recounts an exchange between Coverdale and Jane:

> Sometimes I talked with Miles Coverdale, who seemed to
> sense my feeling of isolation and began to share some of his
> inner self. My admiration for this man grew daily; I won-
> dered at his kindness to me, so much younger and less
> learned, and I marveled at what he had accomplished with
> his life. I was sure that men like Coverdale and Tyndale and
> Latimer would be remembered long after their deaths. I said
> as much to him, but he shook his head, smiling.
>
> "The reward is not in being remembered, Lady Jane, but
> in knowing that while one lives one has 'fought a good fight
> and finished the course' God has set. Why should any of us
> envy another as long as we have been given a particular work
> to do?"
>
> "That is the trouble—not everyone has a task. How can I
> do anything, when all my decisions are made for me from my
> first breath? A man can enter what profession he likes, given
> the intelligence and the will, but a woman—and a gentle-
> woman at that? She makes the most profitable match at the
> earliest possible age and is thereafter expected to cheerfully
> surrender her body, mind, and property. She may not—
> ever—resist the command of a parent or husband."
>
> The chaplain looked sad. "God knows the limitations
> imposed upon us. But he can work around them. . . .
>
> "I was given a bird once, a rare and exotic creature from a
> distant island. But when it was put into a cage, it flew against
> the bars ceaselessly. It refused to accept its confinement and
> eventually damaged itself so badly that it died. I found
> another to take its place. He, too, tried to escape, but after a
> few attempts he settled on his perch. He was a plain fellow, I
> remember, an English sparrow. But my word, Lady Jane,
> how that bird could sing! It was a lesson to me. We can kill
> ourselves, hurling protests against the unfairness of life, or
> we can make the best of who and where we are. Perhaps we
> can even sing."
>
> I gave him a slow smile. "I shall try. Really I shall."[5]

Jane was in far more danger than she knew. While marriage
was the form in which it presented itself, the throne of England

was the object. When she was young, her parents had contracted to marry her to young Edward Seymour, son of the Protector. When the Protector fell from power, and his son was executed along with him, her guardian, Thomas Seymour, planned to marry her to King Edward, her cousin, and successor to Henry VIII. When Thomas fell because of his own scheming, England had a new Protector, John Dudley, Duke of Northumberland. His ambition for Jane was to marry her to his son, Lord Guildford Dudley, which he succeeded in doing, with the cooperation of Jane's parents. Just before young King Edward died, Northumberland persuaded him to "devise" the throne to Lady Jane. "This was to secure succession of a Protestant and also to advance Northumberland's family ambitions."[6]

"Beautiful and intelligent, at sixteen years of age, she reluctantly allowed herself to be put on the throne by unscrupulous politicians."[7] Jane was the titular queen of England for nine days in 1553 before the rightful heir, Henry's Catholic daughter, Mary, claimed the crown for herself, with the support of the people. She confined Jane and her husband to the Tower of London, and in February 1554, they were both executed.

The following prayer is believed to have been written by Lady Jane in 1553.

O merciful God,
Be Thou now unto me a strong tower of defense,
I humbly entreat Thee.
Give me grace to await Thy leisure,
and patiently to bear what Thou doest unto me;
for Thou knowest what is good for me better than I do.
Therefore, do with me in all things what Thou wilt;
only arm me, I beseech Thee, with Thine armor,
that I may stand fast;
above all things, taking to me the shield of faith;
praying always that I may refer myself wholly to Thy will,
abiding Thy pleasure, and comforting myself
in those troubles which it shall please Thee to send me;
and I am assuredly persuaded that all Thou doest
can not but be well;
and unto Thee be all honor and glory. Amen.[8]

2

PLACE

8

A PLACE OF HER OWN

"I was like a rock in a riverbed, looking for a place to belong.
And now I have my wall."

A Philippine Indian, after conversion

You may have seen *Mapp and Lucia* on television, in a drama-tization of E.F. Benson's book. The Lucia novels have a delicious sense of place, as the focus trains on two English villages. Lucia is the reigning monarch of Riseholme and Miss Mapp is the grande dame of Tilling.

These wonderful satires of human behavior contain a sense of completeness; you know that the characters belong, and you find yourself settling into a kind of belonging as you read.

If you ever played king of the castle, you know what these books are about. But instead of king of the castle, we see a struggle about who will be queen of the village. In Riseholme, will it be Daisy or Lucia? And later, in Tilling, will it be Elizabeth Mapp or Lucia?

Beneath the satire of manners of an English village of the 1920s is a power struggle. Who's in charge around here, anyway? Who has the most staying power? Who provides the most entertainments? As you read, you can forget the rest of the world, for everything anyone could want is happening either in Riseholme or Tilling. Life is complete.

Such local color is part of the appeal of Garrison Keillor and his Lake Wobegon lore. We experience a similar small-town life in Cliff Schimmels' novels about Wheatheart, Oklahoma. In our transient world where people move on an average of once every five years, we take some comfort in stories about places where life changes very little and where people cling to their ways as a means of identifying who they are.

What Is Place?
Place is a house or apartment where we live. Place is a neighborhood, a city, a region, a country. Place is a social grouping that is ours, or a relationship that fits. Place is a work in which we feel at home. Place is an aspiration for the future that draws us on to itself. Place is a role that we fill with comfort. Place is the body where we live out who we are. Place is the inner self where we imagine and become.

God knows we need and seek for special places in our daily lives. God's accommodating Himself to our time and space and to our language of location has a long history. In what we call Beginning, God made a place—the Earth. He came to Adam and Eve in the Garden place, at the time of evening. He spoke to Abraham near the terebrinths, the sacred grove of trees where ancient men would expect to hear from deity. He established the holy places and times for the people of Israel, the altar of stones, the tabernacle, the ark, the holy of holies, the temple, the Passover and other festivals, the rituals of sacrifice and belonging.

Today, you and I have our special places, not only for talking to God, but for meeting with one another, for celebrating, for being at home. We have houses and schools and towns that are part of our lives. In its highest sense, though, place is relational. Place is touch, look, smile, laughter, frown, tears, nearness. Place is the bond, the hard-to-define cement between people, that is right or not right.

Houses and Lands
Place is also land. People want land. A place where they and their people belong. This comes through so poignantly in this portion of a letter written by an Indian in Alaska to some missionaries in the area.

I'll go back to my hills and write my songs

and try in what little way I can to preserve,
to reconstruct, to regain a small portion
of that which was once ours by the skyful.
That which is in the trees, the mountains,
the skies, the earth beneath our feet,
the leaves of the grass, the stillness of the waters,
something which people call SOUL.

We see this desire for land in the daughters of Zelophehad.
Their father had died while the Children of Israel were still in
the wilderness. The daughters entered the Promised Land with
their tribe and wanted the privilege of owning land, just as other
families did. Yet, unless the laws of inheritance were changed,
they would have none.

The four women presented a claim which was given to
Moses. He took the claim before the Lord, who responded,
"The claim of the daughters of Zelophehad is good. You must
allow them to inherit on the same footing as their father's
brothers. Let their father's patrimony pass to them."

The Lord then gave Moses instruction about a family with
daughters but no sons, establishing a law which would serve as a
legal precedent for the Israelites. We find this in Numbers 27:1-
11 and Joshua 17:3-4.

When Russian guest Yelena Bonner was about to leave the
United States after a long visit in 1986, she wrote, "I am
convinced that Americans want peace. . . .I maintain that
Americans do not want war. What Americans want is a house.
This desire expresses a national trait, the desire for privacy.
The house is a symbol of independence, spiritual and
physical."[1]

What about the woman alone who all too often is without
land or house? What is home to her? Many single women have a
difficult time thinking of home in a positive sense. They want
home to be a place where they make a nest for husband and
children. Lacking this, they have little interest in the subject.
Some never consider the idea of buying their own place. That is
a thing you do when you get married.

Home is a highly emotional subject. It is the place we come
from and go to, no matter what happens in between. It is the
place where we are alone with our thoughts and dreams, where

we can't avoid the wonderings and the regrets and the hopes that haven't happened yet. Home is the place where we make up our minds about life.

It is important that we feel at home in our homes. And it takes a certain investment in a place before you feel at home there. An investment of effort in making it say *you* and of time in doing things there that express who you are. Home isn't a place to perch. It is a place to dig in and belong.

Living Alone

Making a home by yourself, learning to feel at home where you live . . . these sound simple, and yet they are major challenges for many women alone. Major and worthy. For without meeting these challenges, a woman alone is probably not going to experience a high level of satisfaction in her life.

Living alone is not always easy, especially while you are adjusting to it. When God said it was not good for people to be alone, I think He meant more than the matter of being married. Yet, while it may not be all that good, the fact is that more women than ever before are living alone. The numbers of single adults have changed the shape and size of much of the new construction going on around us.

Some women who will not consider sharing a home might think of being part of a group of friends who are committed to one another and who agree to stay together for a period of years, to provide a caring group for each other.

In the Bible we see examples of single people who used their homes in creative ways. Mary, Martha, and Lazarus were single adults who offered the hospitality of their home to Jesus. Lydia seems to have been a woman alone, and she offered her home as a place for the church to meet and the missionaries to stay. It is thought that many of the meetings of the early church took place in the home of the mother of John Mark. In the days of the prophets, both Elijah and Elisha were given lodging in the homes of widows. One of the loveliest examples of a woman who made herself at home in a strange land is Ruth.

Malla Moe

Some people have an unusual ability to feel at home almost anywhere they are. One remarkable woman of this type was

Malla Moe, the Norwegian-American missionary to Swaziland.

Petra Malena Moe was born on a farm near Hafslo, County Sogn of Fjordane, Norway, on September 12, 1863. She was the eighth child of Calus Rumohr Moe and his wife, Brita Lonheim. In her teenage years, Malla was saved during a revival, as were some other members of her family. When both her parents died and nineteen-year-old Malla was wondering what to do next, a letter came from her married sister Karin in Chicago, asking Malla if she wanted to live with them.

In Chicago, Malla attended Moody Church where she heard D.L. Moody preach. At the close of one sermon, he said, "All Christians get to work, and all sinners come forward." Although she was already saved, Malla stayed to hear more preaching, hoping that she would not be noticed. Moody spotted her, however, and after discovering she was a Christian, challenged her, "If you are saved, then why don't you go to work?"[2]

Later she attended meetings conducted by Fredrik Franson, founder of the Scandinavian Alliance Mission (now TEAM). Franson told Malla, "God wants you to be a missionary in Africa."[3]

Malla was commissioned to go to Africa on April 1, 1892. One bit of final counsel given by Franson at that meeting in New York stuck with her. "Fast and pray," he said. "If you are sick, fast and pray. If the language is hard to learn, fast and pray. If the people will not hear you, fast and pray. And if you have nothing to eat, fast and pray."[4]

Because of Malla's stunning lack of academic and occupational qualifications, it seemed to many that Franson had made a terrible mistake in sending her to Africa. However, his faith in her spiritual qualifications was richly rewarded.

She and her fellow missionaries were pioneers in the days of transporting their few possessions by wagon, of living in huts, of being prey to disease and physical hardship. By September of 1893, their group of missionaries was reduced to three women.

As dark as things seemed just ahead, Malla knew her bridges had been burned behind her. She had now already settled the question of whether to return home. She was utterly useless here, but the Hand was still pushing her forward into the unknown and the impossible. It was in this frame of mind that she conceived a new step. She would not only visit the Swazis in their kraals, but she would make her home among them.[5]

As she followed this resolve during the next years, she made friends with the people, so that some of them called her their White Child and felt sad when she had to leave their kraal.

Malla was not only making friends; she had already cracked the wall of native reserve and, even more than she knew, was starting to work behind it.

It would not be accurate to say that this work in the kraals was done only by Malla, though she started it in Swaziland and carried it on more extensively than any other missionary. What set her kraal work apart was the unique way she did it. Normally the prolonged presence of a white person was enough to create an unnatural atmosphere in a kraal. While there might be courtesy, the very strangeness of the situation was enough to produce a bit of apprehension or suspicion in the Africans.

Malla's special gift was being so human that there was no reason for anybody to be ill at ease. Some other missionaries might sit on their grass mats, sleep in their huts, and eat their food. Malla did it as though she belonged there. Thus she found open hearts as well as open huts.[6]

When someone finally built her a stone house, she named it Bethel, "House of God," after Jacob's story in Genesis 35:3. "It was literally 'home at last' for Malla, for this spot was to be her headquarters and home from that day until her death fifty-six years later."[7]

After ten years in Africa, she returned to the United States for a furlough. It was during this period that she visited in my mother's home in Chicago, since my Norwegian grandparents had interest in Malla's work.

In the years that followed, she continued her treks across South Africa, in the constant challenge of reaching the thousands of kraals where people had not heard about Jesus. Malla would not have been a Calvinist, had she even thought in those terms. She was concerned that her people "keep saved." "She understood something of the pull of heathen culture. She had seen some very promising spiritual children succumb to the pressure of social custom and return to the old life. She was not going to count them secure until she saw them 'safely over.' This was a constant consolation to her when she attended a believer's funeral. 'Now he's safe.' "[8]

In 1927, when Malla was sixty-five, the rigors of constant trekking were beginning to tell on her body. Because she would not consider curtailing her activities, she came up with a new plan—a Gospel Wagon in which she could travel to yet more kraals. This was something like an old-fashioned house trailer, and she traveled in it until 1938.

When Malla was eighty and no longer able to travel in her Gospel Wagon with her group of associates, she still wanted to visit one special place, Bokweni's place. She had been praying for the people there for fifty years. The trip was almost too much for her, but after she had returned home and recovered from the ill effects, she said about it,

"God, He helped me. Not easy. But God, He knows. 'Gladly will I toil and suffer, only let me walk with Thee!'. . . I stayed in a nice hut, slept in a native bed, and I ate food. It was all right, not bad. I thank God for His help. I thank God even if I am old, God still speaks to me and uses me to help people get saved. All grace of God!"[9]

Her home at Bethel was known as the Glory Tea Room. In her later years, the traffic would begin early in the day, people coming to see her.

The woman who cleaned in Malla's house had to have it all finished before daybreak, because that was when the stream of colored folk, Africans and missionaries began to flow through her home, no matter what day. The overflow of guests from the dining room sat in the kitchen, and the surplus from the kitchen had to find places outside the kitchen window.[10]

She would serve tea, and then she would serve dinner, and would be thrilled that her friends were receiving her hospitality. Late in the afternoon, she would serve supper to all who were there. There was always "just one more place." Between the meals would be times of talking of the Lord and encouraging and praying with her friends.

People were coming and going all the time, and some of her fellow missionaries at times felt pressed upon, as if their own work were not of equal importance with hers. As if they had no schedule and could accommodate themselves to her. Reflecting on this later, one of them said,

> "She was impossible at times. She had absolutely no regard for other people's duties." But you're not convinced, even by your own argument. You reach for your Bible . . . and you open to Mark 2 and read: "And it was noised that He was in the house. And straightway many were gathered together . . . and He preached the Word unto them." You read until the twelfth verse, the last seven words: "We never saw it on this fashion."
>
> Your head drops in acquiescence as you answer, "Lord, neither did I—until I met Malla Moe."[11]

In August of 1949, when Malla was eighty-six, a new brick church at Bethel was dedicated. At that point, she had been twenty-eight years without a furlough. She was afraid that if she went home, the Mission Board wouldn't let her return. That year, she went on a series of tours, one requiring a two-hour climb. At eighty-nine, she went on one last trip.

After her death in 1953, many tributes were made to Malla Moe. Among them:

> Her zeal for the salvation of the souls of all people has made her a dearly beloved Mother to many. *Times* of Swaziland, November 28, 1953.

> Whether we are white or black, rich or poor, learned or unlearned, we consider Miss Malla Moe the most outstanding missionary in Africa. Ainsworth Dickson, former Resident Commissioner of Swaziland.

> She . . . blazed the trail, and as she departs today, she leaves Swaziland and the Swazis better than she found them. . . . The history of Swaziland will ever remain incomplete without mention of Miss Moe's name. Iswi Lama Swazi, December 19, 1953.[12]

9

CRY HOMEWARD

The cry that is universal down the ages from all docile hearts which love, which serve, which are alert to greatness, is why, why, why?

Sibyl Harton

Man finds it hard to get what he wants, because he does not want the best; God finds it hard to give, because He would give the best, and man will not take it.

George MacDonald

We live in a world that provokes the question *why*. In the quotation that begins this chapter, Sibyl Harton says that *why* is the cry of all the world, that *why* can be cried in different tones and intensities. At times, it can seem merely an aggravating and long-standing tension of matters that will not resolve. Other times, it can be the wrenching agony of "Why did this happen to me?"

In Ford Maddox Ford's book *The Good Soldier*, which was dramatized on public television, the primary question is, why can't people have what they want in life? The characters, although privileged in possessions and opportunities, are walking tragedies. Some cause harm and others are victims of that harm, for they are all bound together in a deepening confusion and unhappiness.

We hear the universal why as it echoes from Calvary, "My

God, My God, why hast Thou forsaken Me?" Jesus knew why, on an intellectual level. Where He couldn't tell why was in His heart, the place from which we all ask why.

Why do bad things happen to us? Why can't we have what we want? Most of us can answer those questions well enough. We know about free will and choice and life in a fallen world. What our hearts cannot answer is why something bad happened to *us*. Why *we* didn't get what we wanted. Why are *you* alone? Why don't *you* have a husband and children?

The September after my daughter, Catherine, graduated from high school she studied in northern England for six months. This paragraph was in one of her first letters home.

I'm sitting under a big tree on a hill, with Capernwray Hall behind me, another hill with cows grazing in front of me. To one side I can see a castle through the trees, and to the other side is a huge hill. From the top of it, so they tell me, if I look far out to the west, I can see the ocean. I haven't been up there yet. Sometime when I'm feeling particularly homesick, I'll go up there and cry homeward.

What gave that letter special poignancy was that Cathy knew that something she wanted very much at home was in danger. She wanted a stable home where her entire family lived together, and she didn't know what she would find when she returned. She was homesick for a life that was slipping away from her and would become irrecoverable.

As women alone and years older than Cathy, we live with the tension of not having what we think we want—a husband, a shared home. We wonder if we don't matter very much because we don't have what we think we should have, what we felt was promised by someone.

As Christian women, we live with the tension of knowing that we should want the values of the other world, and yet wanting very much some of the good things of this world, and above all desiring to combine the two in a marriage in which we are sure we would serve God very well.

But we are not married, and we wonder if there is, after all, an answer for us. We feel the conflict of living in our bodies and yet being immortal souls. Of trying to make our bodies do the bidding of our souls, and yet being crowded back from what we aspire to do, because of fear of authenticity.

We live with the paradox of wanting to be unique and yet like other people. We live with the desire for the obvious and also for the unavoidable presence of the mystery. For because God has entered our world, nothing can ever again escape bearing His mark. And yet, because He is physically absent, nothing can be quite comfortable.

We live with contradictory values—on the one hand, thinness, youth, consumption, fashion, sophistication, adaptability, self-indulgence, self-definition, self-occupation, cleanliness to a fault. On the other hand, we value sacrifice, surrender, the mystery of God's becoming one of us.

Most of the time we don't think about these tensions. We just feel them, and resent them, for they get in the way of our preoccupation with not having what we want most.

It was the English writer Evelyn Underhill who wrote about "the root of our unrest." A wonderful phrase, and so descriptive of the human condition. Everyone experiences this unrest, regardless of marital status. Evelyn quotes Erigena, a Christian mystic, who said, "The loss and absence of God is the torment of the whole creation; nor do I think that there is any other."[1]

If Erigena is right, and I think he may be, then the presence of God is the delight of the universe. But we do not have Him in body, and we are lonely, and so it is easier to live by the values around us. It is hard to watch and pray. It is hard to wait. It is hard to be different. It is hard to live with the long possibility of not having what we want. Why can't people have what they want? In place of an answer, we have to do something, and so . . .

We go muddling on, knowing we are making a hash of it; people tell us this and that, but somehow they all seem rather like guesses in the dark, and they all fail to be any real use when we come to the bad bits. And at last we realize that only the Author of human life can really teach us to live human life. He alone knows what it is meant to be. And the only way to lay hold of this secret, or to recapture it, is to come to God and be alone with Him.[2]

Women of Two Worlds

I belong to the National Trust for Historic Preservation. In the newspaper that comes monthly, there often appears this quote from John Ruskin: "When we build let us think that we build forever." I read that and sense the tension that no one builds forever, and yet I do care that historic buildings are preserved for posterity.

A few days after the latest paper arrived, I read in Isaiah, "O Lord . . . Thou hast accomplished a wonderful purpose. . . . Thou hast turned cities into heaps of ruin, and fortified towns into rubble; every mansion in the cities is swept away, never to be rebuilt."[3]

I love the Book of Isaiah, filled with mysteries and contradictions as it is. The book begins with a cucumber shed standing alone and ends with a glorious city that will last forever. It begins with a forsaken woman and ends with a loved bride.

God tells the people to rest, and they say, "A little more here, a little there," and "so, as they walk, they will stumble backwards."[4] God invites the people to come back to Him, keep peace, and be safe. But they will not and say, "No, we will take horse and flee . . . we will ride apace." But the Lord waits to show them His favor.[5]

It is a land of vineyards that will not produce until the people pass by the root growing in dry ground. There is a city crowned with everlasting gladness which can be reached only by a causeway for pilgrims, the Way of Holiness.

At the beginning, you see the King not at all, and then only in His splendor, from a far distance. But finally, you see Him close up as the One who delivers from danger and creates delight, who brings to fulfillment and sends peace like a river.

We come to the quenching of thirst in Isaiah 55 only after we confront the Saviour who thirsted and was given vinegar. The bride who in Isaiah 52 prepares herself for her love can reach Him only as the suffering Servant of Isaiah 53. The salvation of Jerusalem can come only after this also, and after the way of justice in chapters 55–59. The comfort of Isaiah 40 is offered only after the chapters of judgment on sin.

We are women of two worlds that connect, and in the Book of Isaiah, which speaks primarily of Israel and of Jerusalem, there are principles that guide us in living in those two worlds.

The bride in the book is the people of God, the new Jerusalem, and cannot be directly compared to a woman alone. But the principles apply. For there is more consistency in the application of principles of Scripture than in the details of specific instances. I am not Deborah or Hannah or Miriam or Lydia, nor do I live in their time. But God is and was and shall be God, and the qualities of His character and the principles of His dealings with people remain the same and are richly interwoven throughout Scripture.

We read of pain and sorrow and rejection and confusion and injustice and want, and God knows all about these. But after a while, there is healing and joy and love and clarity and justice and plenty, and in God's kingdom, these always come in ways that are not on the world's agenda. In God's perspective, the far distance always seems nearer than the close at hand. The tent is more secure than a city.

The Bible is a book of places, of gardens, valleys, mountains and forests, rivers and lakes and seas, of first and last places, of fertile land and waste places, of palaces and threshing floors, of vineyards and deserts and promised lands.

The Bible is a book of future places like Beulah Land and Zion and Mansions in the Father's House and a city with a precious cornerstone for a firm foundation and a river that proceeds from the throne of God and streets of gold and gates of pearl, where God's people will find comfort and feel as fresh as grass in spring.

The Bible is a book of special future for the city Jerusalem, always referred to as a woman, for she will be called by a new name. She will be a glorious crown in the Lord's hand, a kingly diadem in the hand of God. No more will men call her Forsaken, no more will her land be called Desolate, for she will be named Hephzibah or "My Delight" and her land Beulah or "Wedded."

In the psalms, we often see David constructing a house for himself out of anything at hand.

In Psalm 36, we watch him beautifully building towers to heaven with the unfailing love and faithfulness of God, placing ladders to the mountains with God's righteousness, and stairs to the deeps with God's judgments. He finds a place of refuge in the shadow of His wings, and enjoys the plenty of God's house.

He drinks from the flowing stream of God's delight and is bathed with light from the Lord.

As the Apostle John saw the vision of the Holy City, he wrote in most concrete terms of a city with exact dimensions and colors and textures, with a river flowing through and trees growing alongside. In the first chapters of the Bible, we enter a perfect place, the Garden of Eden. All the time and space between Genesis 1–2 and Revelation 21–22 is filled with people who need a sense of place on earth.

But the spiritual sense of place is never missing. When God called Abraham to leave his city and travel to a place which God would show him, he went. When Mary was asked to leave behind the security of a safe life, she accepted the challenge. At-homeness in this world has its values. But so do the moments of homelessness, of belonging to another time and place that is just beyond our reach. For at times we see another form, the likeness of the Son of God walking in the flames with us, moving through our lives alongside us. We reach out for Him, only to be reminded that for now, He is not a God to be held and to be seen with mortal eyes, but to be held in faith and seen with the eyes of the soul.

And when the thing that we want most of all comes to mind and we protest our lack, we are reminded that there may be other things to ask for, that seeking the kingdom comes first, and that all who would be first will be last.

British journalist G.K. Chesterton wrote about the tension between the worlds, about his feeling of being homesick at home, and about his joy when he found that he did not fit into this world.

> The Christian optimism is based on the fact that we do not fit into this world. . . . The modern philosopher had told me again and again that I was in the right place, and I had still felt depressed even in my acquiescence. But I had heard that I was in the wrong place, and my soul sang for joy, like a bird in spring. . . . The knowledge found out and illuminated forgotten chambers in the dark house of infancy. I knew now why grass had always seemed to be as green as the green beard of a giant, and why I could feel homesick at home.[6]

Chesterton asked, "How can we contrive to be at once

astonished at the world and yet at home in it? . . . We need so to view the world as to combine an idea of wonder and an idea of welcome. We need to be happy in this wonderland without once being merely comfortable. . . . One must somehow find a way of loving the world without trusting it; somehow one must love the world without being worldly."[7]

We know Chesterton is right, and yet we want life to be simpler than that. We want to feel at home. But the tension remains, and attaches itself to the things we want most.

Mercy

In the last section of *Pilgrim's Progress*, when Pilgrim's wife, Christiana, and her children are nearing the Celestial City, there is a charming story about Mercy, a young woman who traveled with them and later married Matthew, one of Christiana's sons. Mercy is pregnant with her first child when their company stops in the palace of four shepherds, Knowledge, Experience, Watchful, and Sincere, who entertain the family with what the house affords.

As Mercy looks around the house, she sees something that she would like, but is ashamed to ask for. What she wants is a mirror, and the more she looks at it, the more she wants it, until she asks herself some form of our question, Why can't people have what they want?

When Christiana asks what ails her, Mercy replies, "There is a looking-glass hangs up in the dining-room, off of which I cannot take my mind; if, therefore, I have it not, I think I shall miscarry."

Christiana says that she will ask the shepherds for the mirror. Mercy is ashamed for them to know that she wants something of theirs, but Christiana replies, "Nay, my daughter, it is no shame, but a virtue, to long for such a thing as that."

Christiana speaks to the shepherds and they joyfully grant Mercy her request.

But what was this mirror that Mercy craved, to the threat of miscarriage? It was the looking glass spoken of by Paul and James in the New Testament.[8]

The glass was one of a thousand. It would present a man, one way with his own features exactly; and, turn it but another way, and it would show one the very face and similitude of the Prince of pilgrims Himself. Yea, I have talked with them that can tell, and they have said that they have seen the very crown of thorns upon His head, by looking in that glass; they have therein also seen the holes in His hands, in His feet, and in His side. Yea, such an excellency is there in this glass, that it will show Him to one where they have a mind to see Him, whether living or dead, whether in earth or in heaven, whether in a state of humiliation or in His exaltation, whether coming to suffer or coming to reign.[9]

If we, like Mercy, seek first this looking-glass of life as it is intended to be, there is no chance of our being denied. The mirror does not erase the tension of worlds; rather, it shows us ourselves against both worlds, and fits one against the other in the way God intends.

10

THE KINGDOM OF TOUCH

God's way of loving is the only licensed teacher of human sexuality. God's passion created ours. Our deep desiring is a relentless returning to that place where all things are one. If we are afraid of our sexuality, we are afraid of God.

Richard Rohr

The sex drive presses for immediate satisfaction. It neither knows nor cares for the future.

Bruno Bettelheim

I had met Marcie before, on my travels for work, but I didn't know much about her personal life. Then, one summer evening, after meeting yet another time, she and I went for a walk. As the conversation turned toward our homes, and we exchanged some items about our children, she began talking about her restlessness in being divorced and a single parent. Also, about her discontent at not finding someone suitable to marry. None of that surprised me, for I had heard it from other women.

But when she began recounting the numbers of times she had been propositioned—and by church leaders—I knew I wasn't in for the ordinary. I thought that perhaps she was mistaking their flirtation for something more and I asked her what they said. It seems that they asked for what they wanted in very direct terms. She told me about an affair she had some years ago, with an older man. When she mentioned that he had later married, I inwardly sighed with relief and thought, "Well, that's over. Now maybe she knows better."

But she went on. She feels betrayed by the Lord. "I've prayed for ten years for God to send me a husband and He hasn't. So I am going to get some satisfaction however I can." And she is, currently with a clergyman who comes to her city now and then. She has no illusions about being in love with him. Her motivation is to meet her own needs, which are as much for approval and attention and inner healing as they are for physical satisfaction. She enjoys his interest in her, which she takes as sincere. She says she is tired of feeling guilty, though, and has told him she can't understand how he justifies his actions to himself, since he has a wife and children. His response, "My life with my family is one thing; my work is another, and my personal life is something else."

She knows she will never marry this current man, and hopes that a right one will come along soon. I don't know if she still prays to that effect. I wonder if she thinks that she is the only woman this man sees.

After our conversation, I had two major questions—why she had wanted to tell me the story, and how she could make this square with her Christian beliefs. I never did find out the why, but I discovered the answer to the second question a few evenings later when Marcie and I and two other people were eating together. The table conversation turned to matters of belief, and Marcie began expressing her version of Christianity, which is highly selective, because she believes only those elements of the creeds that she prefers. Her faith is not based on authority, and this explained for me how she can justify her behavior. She does not have a Christianity with a revealed body of truth or an essential atonement for sin. She is quite consistent—she makes up the rules for both her faith and her personal life. Marcie is not comfortable with what she is doing, but those feelings are not strong enough to keep her from pursuing what she wants on her own terms.

A woman alone is in a vulnerable position sexually, whether she has been alone for ten years or ten weeks. Pat, a friend whose husband had taken up with another woman, said he came home one day and taunted her about what she was going to do when he was no longer around. In the context, he meant only one thing. And she felt terribly vulnerable, especially since she had given in to him only the night before.

Marcie and Pat are not unusual. Most women alone struggle with sexual needs. But so do many married women. Temptation comes in such blatant forms, in advertising, in stories, in news items, and in the living arrangements of friends. "In 1970 approximately 523,000 couples in the United States were living together out of wedlock. By 1978 this figure had more than doubled. Recent studies indicate that today perhaps as many as ten million couples are living together outside the bond of marriage."[1]

This estimate doesn't come close to the number of couples who are sexually intimate before marriage but don't live together, or those people who are having extramarital affairs.

According to a 1983 government study, "eighty percent of single American women in their twenties have engaged in sex. . . . One-third of those women have become pregnant at least once, the study says, and forty percent ended their first pregnancies by abortion."

"The report, financed by the National Institute of Health, is the first federal study of the sexual practices of women in their twenties. According to the study, single American women in their twenties have had sex with an average of 4.5 men and one-third of them have lived with a man."[2]

An August 20, 1986 article in the Chicago *Tribune* would be funny if it weren't so sad. The article was entitled, "Fear of Sex—It's Catching" and reported on the changing patterns of "dating" in the Chicago area. Many of those quoted believed that they were on the verge of virginal, since they didn't jump into bed until the sixth or seventh date.[3]

Of Two Minds
One of the most difficult tasks of life is to live comfortably with our bodies. We all need to be loved. We need to love, not only in the general way of wishing people well, or of enjoying their company, but in a highly personal and preferential way of choosing and lavishing and being very exclusive. And our bodies play a major part in our loves. The impulse and ability to love are so good that we don't want them to die

or even diminish. But when warm desire meets up with impossibility, what do we do?

That depends on how we view ourselves, and on what part of us is running the show. Our bodies are very good indeed, but they are not intended to commandeer our souls. When the body takes over, there is no one to assign proper meanings to actions. Thus serial mating becomes little different from what we see in the animal world. The care of the young produced by promiscuous humans is often inferior to what animals provide. Our society is one of throwaway children— one in three children are deserted or thrown out of their homes or taken from incompetent parents. Or, they run away. Add to this one-third the many who are with their parents but in miserable situations, and you have a high number of children who are the victims of irresponsible attitudes toward sexuality. Add to this number all the unborn who were aborted, and you have a frightening statistic about the contemporary expression of sexuality.

When the sex act is separated from a person's sexuality, with all that this involves, it loses its meaning. Any sexual acts should make us more intensely human, in the context of what God intended for human beings to become. A sexual act that is separated from nurture and commitment and love and ongoing care and responsibility has nothing to recommend it except temporary feelings of pleasure.

There are many kinds of love between adults, and not all of them lead to the altar or the bedroom. One of the finest gifts we can offer to ourselves and to the men we know is an expression of warm love that combines friendship and humor and support and appreciation within the context of work or social life—and their marriages, for most of the men we know are married, and if they are happy in their marriages, friendship with them is all the more possible.

Yet this sounds a bit idealistic on the day when you realize that your feelings for a man you work with or see in a social setting have gone far beyond warm friendship or appreciation. What do you do on that day and those that follow? I would suggest several things, the first of which is to assure yourself that you are normal. What you want, love and marriage and care and companionship, are good things. And since you probably don't really want someone else's husband, don't want to cause harm to this man or to his wife and family—or to yourself—your wants are lining up on the right side of the question. And yet you don't know what to do about volatile feelings that threaten to get out of control.

In such a situation, you need to do a good bit of self-talk about the high value you place on marriage, both in principle and in particular, as it applies to this man's marriage. Talk with yourself about the danger of fostering emotional dependence in which life without one person becomes nearly unthinkable. Push yourself into the pursuit of other friendships and activities. Be very careful about what you do and say, so that you don't act in ways that will cause embarrassment when the intense feelings have diminished, as they will.

You can give your feelings and motivations to God and ask Him to hold them and you steady in a time when the ground beneath your feet feels as if it is giving way to clouds and stars. You can make sure you are established on the Word of God as the only adequate foundation for your life. You need defense right now, and society will give you none, and some supposed Christians not much more.

It is important that you weigh the values by which you live. Consider what kind of woman you want to be next year and ten years from now. For every choice you make, every value to which you hold, every moral obligation that binds you—all of these will help you in saying no to temptation. You *can* choose to act against those intense feelings that tempt you to throw over all you have lived by in the past. You *can* choose for the right, when wrong comes dressed in its best clothes. If you have behaved foolishly in the past, you can begin to act in accord with what you know is right. If you have become involved physically, you can make the break. A beautiful young woman I talked with some years ago did just that, though not without deep pain. As she came to understand what it really meant to be a Christian, she knew that she could no longer live with the man she loved, without marriage. He was not a Christian and did not understand why she moved out, when she was still so clearly in love with him. Even as we talked, some months later, her eyes filled with tears as she told me the story, and I felt respect for the obedience to Christ she was living out.

If you find yourself attracted to a good man who is in a less than ideal marriage, you can do a couple of things. First, refuse to listen to complaints about his wife. And second, pray for his marriage. Ask God to draw him and his wife closer to each other, to ease the frictions, to heal the wounds, to help them solve the long problems and to give them a truly good marriage. That you don't feel like praying this way doesn't lessen the validity of the prayer, or of your confidence that this is God's will. You know it is. So you can pray in full faith believing, and put your own discomfort into the prayer as well.

The trouble with so many of us is that we are of two minds when we face temptation. We *don't* want to break up a marriage, and we *do* want to be loved and cared for. The trouble is also in the legitimacy of the need, and in the complexity of male-female friendships. There are good and wholesome levels of friend-love between Christian men and women, and we should never rob ourselves of these. However, when you find that you are becoming emotionally dependent on a man, when you feel that the quality of your life and happiness hangs on his attentions, you have a problem.

Because the man is probably a neighbor, the husband of a friend, or a work associate, you'll want to quietly proceed to make your own life better without radical change in your habits. Don't draw attention to the attraction. If, in a flurry of righteous fervor, you should renounce the error of your ways, you might tip the scale in his already shaky marriage, and wind up with the man on your hands. If you are a follower of Christ, this is not what you want.

Our ability to rationalize is so expansive that we can fool ourselves with the greatest of ease. We all have threads of irrationality and potential imbalances in our personalities. But to foster them draws us away from God and from what is right, and hinders our personal growth.

Sanction of Eros

Sheldon Vanauken writes about what he calls the Sanction of Eros, which he feels is so prevalent in our society. Because something feels right, people tend to think it *is* right.

The Spirit of the Age proclaims sexual love to be the greatest good. In books and films we share the happiness of happy lovers: love itself is lovable. The lovers may experience difficulties—uncooperative spouses and superiors—so that we share their anguish; but the lovers must never face up to the real meaning of betrayal of their vows, for that would mar their happy love. . . . The Spirit of the Age—not the Holy Spirit—ceaselessly proclaims sexual love (or even barnyard sex) to be the ultimate good; and, therefore, anything that stands in its way, solemn vows, duty, loyalty, the words of Our Lord, is seen as chains upon the soaring human spirit.

All thoughtful observers of our society see it to be sex-saturated. . . . But almost no one—neither clergyman nor novelist—really understands this deadly sanction of Eros: the overwhelming feeling that *this* particular love, unlike all others, is right and good and blessed. Young lovers of course feel it, which is why parental opposition to their offspring's choice is rarely successful. And the married man or woman who falls in love with another feels that same Sanction, invariably forgetting that it is exactly what he once felt for his spouse, invariably feeling that this new love is "the real thing at last." And so, because of the Sanction, the seeming blessing from on high, he becomes ruthlessly determined on divorce and remarriage. The Sanction "proves" to him that he is right to break his vows.[4]

Preparing for Temptation
For the average person today, there is something boring about chastity and fidelity. Consider what sells in books, movies, and television. *Little House on the Prairie* and *Sound of Music* may have great nostalgic appeal, but they are not what vast numbers of people want. They are not "interesting." They are not "sophisticated." For many people, forbidden fruit always looks sweeter. The grass on the other side of the fence always seems greener and more lush.

But why is the forbidden fruit more desirable? Why do we wish to walk barefoot on the neighbor's grass? It is not just wanting fruit or grass to walk on. It is also wanting something we know we shouldn't have. James expressed it well when he said that our conflicts "spring from the aggressiveness of . . . bodily desires. You want something which you cannot have . . . you are envious, and cannot attain your ambition . . . you do not get what you want."[5]

Temptation will be more severe for the person who wants to resist evil. If a woman has no real intention of resisting sin, she might as well give in on the first impulse. But for the woman who does intend to live by God's standards, what is there for her? The same thing there is for any serious follower of Christ—a cross and a life of discipline and the filling of the Holy Spirit and the guidance and power of the Word of God.

On the days when temptation moves in with force, it helps if you are ready—if you have already decided a good many things about your behavior, if you have an authority structure in your life, if you know and care about God's standards enough that you will stay with them.

It also helps us to know how Jesus faced temptation. He was led by the Spirit into the wilderness, Satan offered Him things that He wanted very much, and this is the whole point of the temptation. He wanted people to worship Him. He was very hungry. He wanted to be recognized as the Messiah. He wanted to validate His claims. Speaking of the angels must have made Him homesick for heaven.

Jesus met temptation with spiritual resources—with the presence and filling of the Holy Spirit, with deep knowledge of the Word of God, and with an understanding of how God works in this world.

You don't get ready to meet severe temptation the minute after it strikes. That is weeks and months too late. You get ready before, so that when the stress comes, you know what is and is not negotiable. You don't have to waste time and energy wondering whether you should do this or that, or if, in fact, God might really approve of what feels so right.

You help yourself during sexual temptation if you have a well-formulated idea of what it means to be a woman. If, for instance, *woman* means only *sex object*, and you have no other ways in which to define yourself as a woman, it will seem quite feasible to justify immoral action.

You help yourself if you have friends who challenge you and activities that offer you high reward, if your way of life beats boredom most of the time, if you make the most of your natural gifts. The better you feel about yourself, the easier time you will have maintaining your own standards.

You help yourself if you do not compartmentalize your life, if you try to live it in its wholeness, knowing that what you do in one area affects the whole. You cannot get away with riding roughshod over your conscience. You cannot put your beliefs on a shelf to be followed only when you choose to. You cannot live two ways at once for very long.

Human sexuality is a mystery that no one will ever fully understand. Just trying to live comfortably with our bodies is a mystery. That immortal beings are housed in these sometimes awkward and ungainly forms which can behave in such unseemly ways is hard to comprehend. To live at peace with our bodies requires that we have a sense of humor. It probably also requires a fair amount of makeup, and increasing attention to other details as we grow older.

We help ourselves if we remember that life is more than our perception of it. A century ago, a London pastor, Joseph Parker, prayed, "Set upon every believer the stamp of Thy personal majesty."[6]

In time of temptation, instead of saying, "I must have what I want," or "I cannot bear this any longer," we can say, "Lord, You know how bad this feels. Show me meaning. Give me grace. Surround me with protection. Make the purpose greater than the pain, the majesty more than the misery, and keep me in Your will, even when I don't want it."

> If God is holy
> in even one small way
> of dealing in His world,
>
> then He is holy too
> right here and now
> when we want something else,
>
> another way than what this day,
> all scrubbed and shining by His sun,
> is showing off as right.

11

THE SILENCE OF THE WORD

The simple and undisguised emotions of love
are infinitely more expressive than all language,
and all reasoning.

Madame Guyon

When life seems an event unscheduled, marred
by noisy choices made sometime—unruly
offspring of my past—and when all walls
fall down, exposing everything inside,
and I am left bereft, responsible,
they say, for choices that became too loud
and for the ruin that lies around me, then
I listen for the silence of the Word.

CSS

The world of the woman alone is too quiet. There is often no
one near to talk to. But more than that, there is no one close
who cares all that much about what you want to say. You want
to matter deeply to someone. You want to tell your story, in
small parts, but no one wants to hear it. You want to know if
today's part of your story is going to fit the other stories of life
you have lived and heard, and the ones you wish you had heard.
You want to carve your story in stone. And you just may, if no
one wants to listen to what you have to say.

Was it Garrison Keillor who said that many people talk to find out what they think? This kind of talking works better when someone listens. One small part of the story today, another part tomorrow, for we live and tell our story at the same time. We want to live out what we tell, and tell what we live out. And the two come together as hand in glove, so that there is no parting of them.

What we say, we do. What we do, we say. We can't always tell if we are remembering forward or backward, whether we did what we told, or told what we did. We need someone close who will help us remember the order, decipher the meanings, and put them in order of their importance.

If you live alone, you may talk to yourself now and then, and wonder if you are getting dotty or senile. You may flip on the radio or TV when you walk into an empty house or apartment. You may go out to gatherings you don't really enjoy, just to be with people. You may go to malls for the same reason. You may be spending far too much money eating out, for the same reason.

And yet, in all these places, do you find someone who is interested in your story? Who wants to hear the plot line? Who cares about the setting and the progression of scenes? Who wants to know the characters?

In *The Fish Can Sing*, by Finnish novelist Halldor Laxness, the young boy Alfgrim wants to hear a famous singer from his town perform. Alfgrim is seeking to find his way in life, and thinks he might pursue music. As he asks his grandmother if they will all go to the concert, she senses his need.

> "Oh, I don't think we'll be going down to Austurvoll to hear a song we cannot hear at Brekkukot, my child," said my grandmother.
> "In that case, I'll go by myself," I said.
> "Do that," she said. "In any case, I have already heard my own song. Yes indeed. But you have yet to hear your song. On you go. And attend to God, as my grandmother used to say."[1]

To hear your own song, to get hold of the title you can put on the marquee—"Wife of . . . " "Mother of . . . " But it didn't work out that way, and you may still be struggling to find the theme of your life story. To make sense of the plot line that is

93

happening in and around you and seems so senseless. A story no one would buy.

When life isn't making much sense, when the words aren't coming together in a coherent tale, the very vowels and consonants sound noisy. The words create more distance between people. When we aren't saying things that create closeness, we still feel the need to say something, to fill the emptiness, and what we say falls on our own ears as false. We know it isn't right. We know it doesn't speak from the heart. And we don't always know how to remedy the problem.

We live in a noisy society. Our cities are overcrowded. Mechanization is noisy. The media are noisy. Added to the noise from the outside is the noise from inside ourselves. We are trying to deal with too much information, with too much stress, with a pace that propels us faster than we want to go. Too much is happening and the dissonance level rises . . .

And then we go to church and hear about the Word of God, the spoken and written Word, and the incarnate Word. We sing about the creative Word of God. We hear about the redemptive Word, and we wonder . . . what has all that really to do with the sounds and silences in my life? How do these relate to the fact that there is too much noise and not enough significant sound? Too much activity and not enough presence?

In his book *The Humiliation of the Word*, Jacques Ellul writes about the living quality of words.

Speech is basically presence. It is something alive and is never an object. It cannot be thrown before me and remain there. Once spoken, the word ceases to exist, unless I have recovered it. Before it is spoken, the word places me in an expectant situation, in a future I await eagerly. The word does not exist on its own. It continues to exist only in its effect on the one who spoke it and on the one who recovered it. . . . Dialogue involves the astonishing discovery of the other person who is like me, and the person like me who is different.[2]

When we think of Christ as the Word, we are reminded of Paul's words, "Let the Word of Christ dwell in you richly." For that Word to dwell in me, Christ must be the One I can discover in dialogue—the person like me, yet different. There has to be something in common for me to understand and give place to IIis words.

Yet, what does it mean to let the Word of Christ dwell in us richly? And what does this have to do with the overly quiet life of the woman alone? In the Book of Hebrews are familiar words that contain so much meaning I wonder if I shall ever know it all.

> For the Word of God is alive and active. It cuts more keenly than any two-edged sword, piercing as far as the place where life and spirit, joints and marrow, divide. It sifts the purposes and thoughts of the heart. There is nothing in creation that can hide from Him; everything lies naked and exposed to the eyes of the One with whom we have to reckon.[3]

That place where soul and spirit divide, where joints and marrow separate, has long been regarded as the center of the self. The place where the inner person resides. The place of the inner kingdom of God, of which Jesus spoke. That inner region which is impossible to see and difficult to understand. And yet it is here that God promises to meet with us. It is here that we are to let the Word of Christ dwell richly. It is here that the riches of the inheritance are to be worked out in our experience. It is here that the Sword of the Word does its cutting work of correction and comfort and creation.

Madame Guyon

One woman who felt the cutting of the Word in a special way was Madame Jeanne Marie Bouvier de la Motte Guyon. She was born in April of 1648, at Montargis, France, and was educated mostly in convents. At the age of sixteen, she was married to a rich man twenty-two years older than she. Already in her young life, she had shown a bent toward spirituality and found herself very unhappy in the worldly atmosphere of her husband's home. She was particularly miserable to have to live in the same household with her husband's mother, whom she regarded as a most difficult woman.

Between 1664 and 1676, she bore five children and lost one son and one daughter in death. Her sister died, as did her mother and father. She recovered from a serious illness in 1666, but in 1670, she contracted smallpox and was left disfigured.

Because she was a beautiful woman, people thought she would be inconsolable. But she said,

> As I lay in my bed, suffering the total deprivation of that which had been a snare to my pride, I experienced a joy unspeakable. I praised God with profound silence. . . . When I was so far recovered as to be able to sit up in my bed, I ordered a mirror to be brought, and indulged my curiosity so far as to view myself in it. I was no longer what I was once. It was then I saw my heavenly Father had not been unfaithful in His work, but had ordered the sacrifice in all reality.[4]

In 1676, her husband died, leaving her with a comfortable inheritance. As her charitable works continued, and her teachings on prayer and the spiritual life became more popular, the religious authorities grew jealous, and from 1695 to 1702, she was in and out of prison, until she was taken ill and Louis XIV released her to her son's home.

Madame Guyon nursed the poor, established hospitals, gave alms, and wrote more than forty books, including a 700-page autobiography and *Spiritual Torrents*, a book "teaching the way to the true silence of the soul."[5] She was considered a leading proponent of Quietism. "Her chief mission was to teach that holiness is based on faith. She felt that she had been sent to teach a weary world effective methods of prayer."[6]

Her teachings were based on her understanding of the inner place. In her younger years, as she sought to live a life of prayer before God, she found herself frustrated, until a young Franciscan gave her direction for her spiritual life. "Your trouble comes from seeking externally what all the time is within you. Accustom yourself to seek God in your own heart, and you will find Him there."[7]

She believed that we all have access to God "who dwells at the 'fine point' of each human spirit."[8] The point where the Word cuts through soul and spirit, joints and marrow. The place where the silent sound of the Word confronts the interior noise of a life that has not yet found rest.

Madame Guyon came also to see this inner place at the center as a table, reflecting Thomas à Kempis, whose *Imitation of Christ* she had read. He had written, "Without Thee my table is empty."[9]

She said, "The table is the center of the soul; and when God is there, and we know how to dwell near, and abide with Him, the sacred presence gradually dissolves the hardness of the soul, and, as it melts, fragrance issues forth."[10]

The Table of Inwardness

The table is a lovely picture of the inner kingdom, and so much more visual than the unseen membrane that separates soul from spirit, that leads right to the central point of who I am as a person. I am a mystery to myself much of the time, as you are to yourself. And only infrequently does someone else really come close to touching the very center of our beings.

But God can. Through the Word, both written and lived out in Christ, He penetrates our natures, cuts to the essence of who we are, reaches under the layers of old hurts and excuses, pulls at habits that are harmful, points out behaviors that are getting in the way of growth.

For when it comes down to cases, there is only One who can really understand all that happens in you, in me, for there is only One who sees all—the One who made us. He knows our names, He cares about our stories, He understands our past and our future, and He comes alongside us to help and to lead us, to wipe away our tears and to make all new. This is the One who wants us to be the women He sees we can become.

In the inner place where God does His divine surgery, in this place where we decide what we will be, we can respond or we can ignore. We can grow or we can stagnate. We can change or we can rust. We can admit or we can make excuses.

And if we choose to listen for the voice of God, we may hear in a dark place, "Let there be light." In a fallow place, "Let there be fruit-bearing trees." In a vulnerable place, "Let there be walls of protection." In an anxious place, "Let there be peace." And we will sing our songs, the ones we hear deep inside our souls, when we sit at the table with our Host, and we will wonder at their likeness to what we are coming to know ourselves to be.

The longer you sing your song, the more often you will think that you hear an echo of something like the melody you are singing. And the more you eat at His table, the more accustomed you will become to His ways and His supply for your soul. Calvin Miller said it this way:

> The table in the wilderness is a place of unceasing relationship. Our togetherness with Christ is far more than an intermittent prayer life. Rather, it establishes a strong bridge with two piers, one driven in time, and the other in eternity. . . . Ours is a quiet meal. Our Host sits with us at a table whose silence is the center of our hearts.[11]

When we learn how to live with the Word of Christ deep in the center of our being, we will know the creative Word who was in the beginning with God, and who will be at the end of time with God. We will know the cohesive Word who holds everything in the universe together. We will know the redemptive Word by whom we were washed from our sins to a new life. We will know the sustaining Word who gives support to all that is.[12]

And we will know that we have taken into our hearts so much more than words and silences. For we are finding out who we are, from the One who made us to be who we are. We are forgetting to say dull words whose only purpose was to fill the quietness. We are remembering to seek the silence that is filled with words of goodness and future and love. And we are discovering a kind of care in the penetrating Word .that surprises, for we didn't expect sympathy and grace and mercy along with the cutting Word . . . We didn't expect One who was like us.

> Since therefore we have a great high priest who has passed through the heavens, Jesus the Son of God, let us hold fast to the religion we profess. For ours is not a high priest unable to sympathize with our weaknesses, but one who, because of His likeness to us, has been tested in every way.[13]

12

THE LONG WORD

Commitment, curious paradox,
where all of life is mine in so much as His cross is mine,
where I am free to build confining walls about us,
walls of purpose, love, integrity;

where I receive according as I give,
wherein I tire, and yet find rest in that which wearied me,
where I seek knowledge that God gives
in ways to force awareness of my own incompetence;

where, catapulted into seeming chaos,
I can rest, cared for by a lasting love,
and cradled in security I could not find
without commitment to unseen realities.

CSS

As a woman alone, you fill certain roles. You may be worker, friend, daughter, mother, sister, aunt, grandmother, committee member, participant in a sport or hobby, chairperson, volunteer in church or community.

Over a lifetime, most of us fill many roles, and unless we stop to look at them, we may view them as random selections of activities and associations that have little connection. However, when we take the long look at our roles, we begin to see a pattern, not only of friendships and interests, but also of values and commitments. Over a period of years, the prime role functions of our lives will connect with a line that runs through the center of our loyalties to ideas and to people.

Roles are places where we play out our loyalties, where we keep our commitments, where we carry out our convictions, and where we reflect our personhood. It is important that we not allow ourselves to be cast into new roles that are not reflective of our commitments, not natural to our abilities and goals, and that do not offer some aspect of growth, for us or for other people.

Andrew Greeley's Chicago-based novels have taken a drubbing from critics. One favorite word to describe the books is "steamy," and certainly there is an element of steam. But some of the books are more than that. As Greeley himself said on a television appearance on Oprah Winfrey's talk show in June of 1986, "I think my readers recognize that these are books of faith and commitment and love."

I was intrigued with the format of *Thy Brother's Wife*, for the eight sections of the book are introduced with verses from the Upper Room discourse and prayer of Jesus, before His crucifixion. In his introductory note, Greeley writes, "On Holy Thursday, while eating the unleavened bread of the Seder with His followers, Jesus committed Himself to them irrevocably." In his afterword, Greeley wrote, "This particular religious story will be successful if the reader is disconcerted by a tale of commitments that are imperfectly made and imperfectly kept—but that are still kept. And by the image of a God who draws straight with crooked lines, who easily and quickly forgives, and who wants to love us with the tenderness of a mother."[1]

As I looked at the verses Greeley quoted in his section pages, I saw that in Jesus' words in the Upper Room, He gave His followers the three elements we are talking about in this book. He gave them a Person, Himself, when He said that He called them to be His friends. He offered them a place that He said He would prepare for them. And He offered them purpose and a specific work and way. He was the way, and their primary work would be to love one another.[2]

Long Commitment

Something that has been missing from the contemporary scene in recent years is long commitment. The current notion seems to be that we stay with something as long as it is easy.

I know as well as anyone that there are times when we are not able to keep major commitments of our lives. But those times should be rare. I know also that there are times when we are pressed to choose between one commitment and another, because something happening in our lives makes it impossible to keep both of them. This a most painful choice that should be made only as a last resort. For we will make few long-term commitments in our lives, to specific people or groups, or to dominant goals and ideas that lead us. But those few commitments should be well considered and kept, as far as is humanly possible.

In the Bible we see people who struggled through years and decades of commitment to God's promise or directive, even though they could not see the result. Chapter 11 of Hebrews is a record of the faithful who sought for a city but did not find it, who put their money on faith instead of putting faith in their money. Hebrews 11 is touted as our list of heroes, but I wonder how comfortable we would feel around the people mentioned. They were so uncommonly determined and stubborn, and insistent that they had a word from God that bound them to something they could not see.

Today we have that Word in forms they could only imagine. We have the prophetic Word in which they lived, and we have the presence of the Incarnate Word and the written Word. And yet, the more we have of something, the less we tend to value it. The more words, the less meaning they seem to have. And sometimes this devaluation can wend its way into our understanding of that higher Word which is not relative, not locked into time and place, and not stored in the computer.

The Word that is above all words is alive and active, the communication of one who called Himself the Word and who wants to be a vital and verbal part of our lives. Yet His words so often call us away from the status quo.

We all like to have roles to fill, for they are a comfort. They are a defense against having to make up our minds every day about what we will do. They save us time and energy and help us to focus our lives.

However, it can be in this place of roles that the woman alone has trouble. She may not like the roles she feels are pushed on her by other people. She may feel trapped, like a person without enough options. She may need to remind herself that her role is something she fills, she chooses. She does not have to be and do what others expect of her.

In the area of roles, the woman alone has great flexibility. She is free to become, to do, to move, to stay, to combine role functions, to make minor or major changes.

But such role adaptation takes courage and imagination. It requires your belief in your story, your song, your part in the play. It means that you, at least, must listen to your own story, and know the motivations of the main character—you. It means that you must know what you most want. It means that you have to deal with your commitments to God, and even more, His commitments to you.

Incredibly Proper

When we Americans think of role fulfillment in society, we tend to think of the British, for throughout their history, they have known and played their roles so well that we who prize our democratic "equality" will stay up half the night to watch one of the royals be married. In 1986, when Prince Andrew and Sarah Ferguson were married, the Sloane Rangers were in the news, because Sarah was one of them. The Sloane Rangers? The British equivalent of yuppies. Market researcher Peter York claims to be the one who discovered the Sloanes back in 1970. He says that the Sloane Ranger Handbook he and Ann Barr wrote was the first English lifestyle book. The Sloanes fit into one of the precise social groupings that have traditionally been easier to identify in Britain than in America, because people there tend to stay in their own classes. However, this is changing.

The old upper-class Tories, the wetter Macmillan generation, would never have been comfortable with the flaunt-it Eighties. Play it down was their watchword. Their sense of class was more mystical. Nowadays we're moving from this towards the American lifestyle way of class which allows for the war of all against all. But we're moving very slowly.

The new American system puts a subtle pressure on us. Now people feel that if they're not clever, beautiful, rich and famous, something's gone wrong. There's one thing to be said for the old system, for knowing your place. It reduces anxiety. It may be why, in a recent international happiness survey, Britain came out top.[3]

But let's go back a few generations in British history, to days of less anxiety, in the time of William Wilberforce, when people said things like, "What business has a bishop got being religious?" Earlier yet, when the anxiety level was even lower—at least, among those who were counted—in the time of John Wesley and his brother, Charles, and also of George Whitefield and the beginnings of Methodism. For in this severely partitioned society, the upper class was aghast at what they called "the great unwashed," the coal miners and other laborers who

did not know how to behave or how to talk; they did not know or care who Horace was, or what Maecenas said to him. The chilly rationalism of the Anglican religion took no hold on their lives. All they had was sinful human hearts and obscure human feelings. The upper classes hardly recognized those attributes in themselves at all.

A nice story is told of an eighteenth-century lady, who was advised by her gamekeeper of a gathering of Methodists outside the gate beyond her park. A footman was sent out to learn what they were doing, and returned to say that they were praying for her ladyship. "Really," she said, with a sniff of disdain, "Things have come to a pretty pass when religion starts interfering with a person's private life."[4]

Lady Huntingdon

Selina Shirley married Theophilus Hastings, the ninth Earl of Huntingdon, on June 3, 1728, and became the Countess of Huntingdon. They lived at Donington Park in the parish of Castle Donington in Leicestershire. In the following years she and the Earl had seven children, and she became known as Lady Bountiful for her works of charity. "She was a lady of breeding, born to command, and she must have made a striking picture with her large expressive eyes, pretty mouth and noble forehead."[5]

When she was thirty-nine, she was taken seriously ill, and it was during this time that she was brought to a personal faith in Jesus Christ. She had for some years sought to prove herself worthy of heaven and to quell her doubts, but she could not. It was after a sister-in-law, Lady Margaret Hastings, told her of hearing an evangelical preacher and of coming to know her own sins forgiven that Lady Selina asked, "Is it possible? An assurance that, come what may in life, I am one of God's elect? That my faults are all forgiven and written off from the Book of Life? If I trusted completely in the Lord, would I have an assurance like Margaret's?"

Selina closed her eyes and prayed ardently, "Lord Jesus, come into my heart. Take charge of my life. I am Yours to command and I will obey."

Directly she felt a sweet peace surge through her. She no longer ached and she rested quietly. She had received that assurance. Come what may, Jesus was her Saviour and Master.[6]

It was in the years following this experience that Lady Selina began to be involved in the evangelical movement. Then in 1743 she lost two children and in 1746 her husband died. "Although she was left a very wealthy woman, Lady Huntingdon resolved to use her means to further the cause of the Gospel of her Saviour. Keeping enough to provide food, lodging, and the education of her children, she invested her inheritance in those who would help further her mission."[7]

In 1748, she invited Whitefield to preach at her house in Chelsea, and also at her homes in London, Brighton, and Bath. During this year, she and her daughters and several preachers made a mission trip into Wales to bring the Gospel to remote villages. In 1750 and following, she exercised her right as a peeress to appoint as many chaplains as she pleased.

It was about this time that Whitefield said to her, "A leader is wanting. This honor has been put on your ladyship by the great Head of the Church."[8] Another Methodist leader, Dr. Philip Doddridge, said of her, "I think I never saw so much of the image of God in a woman upon the earth."[9]

It became all the rage for people of high position to form parties to hear different preachers. Among those who came to Lady Huntingdon's home to hear Whitefield were Scottish philosopher David Hume, author Horace Walpole, Lord Bolingbroke, and Lord Chesterfield. "Bishops of the Church of

England came incognito and sat in a curtained recess dubbed 'Nicodemus Corner.' Women of high position flocked to hear the new minister too, and soon other mansions of the rich resounded with the new interpretation of the Gospel."[10]

In 1760, when George III took the throne, the moral state of the Empire was very low. "Now was the time for Lady Huntingdon to take an even more active role in reviving her beloved country and church."[11] In 1761, she built her first regular chapel at Brighton, financed by the sale of her jewels. Later she built other chapels, in Tunbridge and London.

Also in 1761, she saw the beginning of the Countess of Huntingdon "Connexion," a much wider association of preachers beyond the Wesleys and Whitefield, so that the Gospel cause could be furthered throughout the land.

In 1768, she founded a seminary at Trevecca in Wales, to provide training for preachers of the evangelical persuasion. Whitefield was there to officially open the school on Lady Selina's sixty-first birthday.

After the one-year celebration of the school, in 1769, Lady Selina wrote, "Oh that I may be more and more useful to the souls of my fellow creatures. I want to be, every moment, all life and zeal, all activity for God, and ever on the stretch for closer communion with Him. My soul pants to live more to Him, and be more holy in heart and life, that all my nature may show forth the glories of the Lamb."[12]

On his death in 1770, Whitefield bequeathed to her an orphanage in Georgia. In 1772, she sent missionaries from Trevecca to America.

Although Lady Huntingdon became more and more closely identified with the Methodist movement, she wanted to stay in the Church of England and was a member when she died. She used her social position to further her religious purposes. When her cause failed in a church dispute with the Archbishop of Canterbury over the rights of her chapels, she took her case to King George III and Queen Charlotte. After they had finished with the church matters, she stayed to converse on other topics. The king said to her,

"I have been told so many odd stories of Your Ladyship, that I am free to confess that I felt a great degree of curiosity to

105

see if you were at all like other women. I am happy to have the opportunity of assuring Your Ladyship of the very good opinion I have of you, and how very highly I estimate your character, your zeal and abilities, which cannot be consecrated to a more noble purpose."[13]

Because she had financed so much of the work from her own funds, she wanted to establish means by which the Gospel work could continue, and so she formed an association into which she channeled her money, to be used for the same purposes after her death.

When she died in June of 1791, she had outlived all of the early Methodist leaders. She had lived forty-five years after her husband's death—and never got over missing him. In her years alone, she devoted the resources of her strong personality, her money, her high social position, her deep devotion to God, and her energies and vision into the Gospel ministry.

Lady Selina could have chosen to conform much more closely to what society expected of her as a peeress, instead of responding to the call of God. But she saw her role in society as a resource she could use in God's service, and she employed it faithfully and with imagination and creative leadership.

None of us will fill the role that Lady Selina did. But the question never is whether we have the way of life of someone else. We are each responsible for what we have, not for what we might have had in another time and place.

In any age, the question always is whether we will choose comforts over commitments, lifestyle over the persistence of the long word that makes itself heard throughout our lives.

Jacques Ellul has a fine phrase, "the order of evident things," in which I see the way our roles express our deep commitments. For in the roles we assume over a period of time, there is an order of evident things, so that what is not at first seen becomes evident because of the order of our lives.

And the curious paradox? Only that any serious commitment does curtail our choices. When we decide for one thing, we have decided against many others. And yet there is freedom in the order of a committed life, which becomes more evident as time goes on and as compounded choices work together into a wonderful unity of person and work.

13

THE HOUSE OF YESTERDAY

If there is a wall between you and the world,
it makes little difference whether you describe yourself
as locked in or as locked out.

G.K. Chesterton

Life can only be understood backwards;
but it must be lived forwards.

Søren Kierkegaard

Near the town of Fenimore, Wisconsin, on a corner of two country roads, is a shop called The House of Yesterday, a place for finding antiques and memories of days gone by.

As I saw the shop, I thought how we all have our houses of yesterday and how those houses just won't stay in one place, but follow us everywhere we go. We forget about them periodically and think to enter a new situation in full contemporary style, a woman of today, when suddenly we hear a wheeze from the past and turning, see our house chugging into place beside us.

The house of yesterday? An old structure with sturdy walls and high ceilings, a house of many rooms, filled with antiques and memories, filled with a past that is personal to you, to me, and something we can't escape even if we would.

Some women have not only house but barn and coach house and fences and brick walls six feet high, so that no matter where they go, they are walled off either from themselves or from the world. For within those personal walls are old habits, relationships that continue to mirror inadequacy, feelings of insecurity, aloneness, boredom, rejection, as well as some truly good things that are part of life past.

Within those walls are the ghosts of family past and ethnic ways and physical limitations and strengths. For some, within those walls is the feeling that home is a place you stay only when you have nothing better to do, and so the walls become a prison, a holding cell for waiting until the morning comes with hope that even yet a man may make his way into your house of yesterday and exorcise the ghosts of all that was and somehow still remains.

It was Robert Frost who said, "Something there is that doesn't love a wall, that wants it down." To be walled in can make us claustrophobic, unable to breathe. To be walled out can make us angry and feel victimized by life.

What are we to think about those walls in the house of yesterday? We cannot live without them. We can't make them go away. Nor would we want to entirely, for life needs restrictions, definitions, perimeters, dimension, shape.

Without walls, we would be forever making decisions that would leave us no time to act. The very restrictions of our lives can offer us the freedom to pursue what is possible within their confines. At times we may try to scale a wall, go around another, or take one down. But never all of them.

Walls are backgrounds against which we live our days. To one woman, an old stone wall is an outdated relic and something to ignore. To another, the old stone wall is a place to plant a rock garden and make a refuge of quiet beauty. Walls are what we make of them.

Our bodies are walls around our spirits, and the color of skin and hair and eyes, the shape of nose and mouth, the size of hands, and the tallness or shortness, thinness or stoutness, all are bricks in that wall. Our wealth or poverty, our level of education, our physical health and energy level, our beauty or plainness, our giftedness, all are bricks in our wall.

Everything in this world has boundaries. Everything is circumscribed by barriers. When God began to make a world, He set about establishing distances and differences and distinctions and constructing walls. The very atmosphere around our world is like a bandshell to protect us and make possible life on what we call the earth.

In our individualism, we want a "Don't Fence Me In" freedom. "Don't get in my space. Don't restrict me." And while this tendency can be amusing and seemingly freeing, it can carry over into our personal perceptions of possibilities and relationships, so that we don't want any restrictions except those of our own choosing. This is not possible.

As women alone, we live with cultural and social barriers that are often uncomfortable. We live with too much aloneness in our house of yesterday, so that we can fail to open wide its windows to this day and to the future. We can sit in a musty house of memories and feel sorry for ourselves and blame people and concentrate on what was supposed to be but never happened. Or on what happened and fell apart.

Or we can measure the walls that are there for keeps, decide which ones should be taken down, which need a door or window in them, and then slowly begin to make changes.

When we pray, we are often conscious of the barriers in our lives. And in our prayers, we have choices to make. We can beat upon the walls that seem to hem us in, or we can breathe the very freedom of God into those walled places and let the fresh breezes cleanse away the mustiness. We can rebel against what is not, or we can choose to use what is. We can ignore the house of the past, or we can decide to embellish and refurbish and beautify the old, polishing to a shine what has value, moving one memory to stand alongside another, rearranging the relative importance of events in our past.

We can sit in the hallway of our house and say, "If only," or we can actively live in all the rooms, and bring together the very best of yesterday and today.

Walls of Impossibility

In the Bible we meet people who were up against stone walls until God came along. The circumstances in Job's life didn't change during the story. Yet in the first half of the book, he was walled out of life and in the last chapters he possessed the world. The difference? He had seen God.

The Old Testament hero of faith, Rahab, came to know the

wall of Jericho as a place of deliverance for her and her family. That wall was going to lead to the destruction of her neighbors. But for her, it would mean salvation.

Esther was walled in literally and symbolically when Haman persuaded her husband, King Ahasuerus, to sign a decree against the Jewish people. And yet that barrier of impossibility became her opportunity to work for good.

Sarah lived with the frustrating barrier of barrenness, until God decided it was time for her to bear a child.

Peter was walled in in a prison, until the angel came and led him to freedom. Paul and Silas were walled in in a prison, until the angel freed them first in their hearts, then from their chains, and later from the walls.

But God does not always rescue people from the walls of difficulty. Joan of Arc was cornered by her own confession of faith. She could have recanted and gone free, but to do so would have meant such a loss of real freedom that she chose rather to die. Sir Thomas More and Thomas à Becket fell against the walls of dogma and lost their lives to the caprice of kings, or so it seemed. In actuality, they chose to stand with truth as they understood it.

In the Book of Jonah, in the Berkeley version, is a verse I only recently noticed. "Those who revere worthless idols give up the grace that might be theirs."[1] I connect this with the past and with barriers that seem to cut us off from what we want. For we can come to idolize what we don't have, what we think we deserve, what might have been, if only . . . And when we love our victimized state more than God's good purposes for us, we surely do give up on the grace that might be ours, for we have nothing in which to receive that grace. Our hands are busy with worthless idols.

Canadian writer Margaret Clarkson identifies another kind of wall, a hedge of God's purposing.

Hedges are thorny; hedges are sharp; hedges are thick and high . . . hedges shut life out and shut pain, fear, and loneliness in. Misunderstanding and frustration thrive within their prickly walls. . . .

But—God's hedge! The hedge of His purposing, His planting, His tending—this makes all the difference. . . .

For those who believe in the love and wisdom of a sovereign God, who see His hand in all that concerns them, a God-hedged life, if a somewhat awesome, even a terrible thing, can be wonderful—a life of joy and freedom, a life of peace and praise. . . .

The hedge can cut off the world and confine on every side, but it cannot . . . prevent the soul from looking up into the face of God. . . .

If we would know the dew of God's presence within our hedges, however, we must be sure that our barriers are not of our own making. . . . God has made a hedge about the life of every believer. The thorns that seem to hem us in are in reality placed there to close us in to God Himself, to protect us from evil, to provide us with sanctuary in the midst of a troubled world.[2]

Sojourner Truth

Before the Civil War, the American nation was divided by the issue of slavery, and the people who could never escape the issue and its consequences were the slaves themselves. During this period of time, several remarkable Negro women came to prominence because they caught the vision of a free spirit and saw the possibility of what they and their people could become. They could not undo the wall of color, but they could leap over the wall so that they became a blessing and a challenge to many. Amanda Smith became known as a missionary and an evangelist. Harriet Tubman was called the Moses of her people, as she led over three hundred slaves to freedom in the north, along the route of the underground railroad.

Sojourner Truth's owner named her Isabella Baumfree when she was a girl. She was sold twice, the second time to a farmer who raped her and then married her to another slave by whom she had five children. She was later freed and joined a religious community. She believed God had told her to become an evangelist against slavery. So she started out to be an itinerant preacher, changing her name to Sojourner Truth, because the Lord "had told her that she was to be a sojourner—a wanderer on earth—and to carry His truth to all who would listen."[3]

Sojourner became a compelling speaker. She would carry

banners in her pockets and then set them up to attract an audience. "I sets up my banner, an' then I sings, an' then folks always come up round me an' then I preaches to 'em. I tells them about the sins of His people. A great many always come to hear me; an' they're right good to me, too, an' say they want to hear me agin'."[4]

White people were anxious to hear a black person speak, and especially a slave. The black orators were eager to oblige them, and Sojourner and Harriet Tubman were two of the greatest ex-slave orators.

Illiterate, their tradition was an oral one, their consciousness was oral. They spoke in singing cadences with all the expressiveness of the black tongue. The Southern black had a quality that even the most eloquent white speaker lacked— an ability to speak immediately, poignantly, without any sense of an intervening censoring self-consciousness.[5]

When Sojourner came to know about God, her knowledge was incomplete. She felt the need of someone to stand between her and an offended God. So she looked for someone, and claimed that Jesus made Himself known to her. He was so good and "so every way lovely, and He loved her so much! And, how strange that He had always loved her, and she had never known it! And how great a blessing He conferred, in that He should stand between her and God. And God was no longer a terror and a dread to her!"[6]

She contemplated the unapproachable barriers that existed between herself and the great of this world, as the world calls greatness, and made surprising comparisons between them, and the union existing between herself and Jesus—Jesus, the transcendently lovely as well as great and powerful; for so He appeared to her, though He seemed but human; and she watched for His bodily appearance, feeling that she should know Him, if she saw Him; and when He came, she should go and dwell with Him, as with a dear friend.[7]

During the early years, she thought she was the only one who had found Jesus, and that He loved only her. She felt that if others came to know and love Him as she did, she should be thrust aside and forgotten, being herself but a poor ignorant slave.

She gradually came to understand that Jesus loved all people. Although her theology was a bit confused on some points, she loved Jesus and was a faithful witness for Him. When Henry Ward Beecher asked Sojourner if she preached from the Bible, she replied that she couldn't read a letter. She had just one text, "When I found Jesus."[8]

On one occasion she shared the speaking platform with Frederick Douglass and Wendell Phillips. Douglass, carried away by his recital of the wrongs done to the slaves, ended "by saying that they had no hope of justice from the whites, no possible hope except in their own right arms. It must come to blood, they must fight for themselves, and redeem themselves, or it will never be done."

When Douglass finished, a huge hush fell over the house and Sojourner's voice sounded out: "Frederick, is God dead?"

"The effect was perfectly electrical, and thrilled through the whole house, changing as by a flash the whole feeling of the audience."[9]

Harriet Beecher Stowe, author of *Uncle Tom's Cabin*, said of Sojourner,

I do not recall ever to have been conversant with anyone who had more of that silent and subtle power which we call personal presence than this woman. . . . She was dressed in some stout, grayish stuff, neat and clean, though dusty from travel. On her head she wore a bright Madras handkerchief arranged as a turban, after the manner of her race. She seemed perfectly self-possessed and at her ease—in fact, there was almost an unconscious superiority, not unmixed with a solemn twinkle of humor, in the odd composed manner in which she looked down on me.[10]

In the 1850s, Sojourner settled in Battle Creek, Michigan. At the beginning of the Civil War she gathered supplies for Negro volunteer regiments and in 1864 went to Washington, D.C., where she helped integrate streetcars and was received at the White House by President Abraham Lincoln. The same year she accepted appointment with the National

Freedmen's Relief Association, counseling ex-slaves, particularly in matters of resettlement. As late as the 1870s, she encouraged a substantial migration of freedmen to Kansas and Missouri. In 1875, she returned to Battle Creek, where she remained until her death in 1883.[11]

Breaking Through Barriers

Every woman lives with barriers and walls of some kind. It is easy to look on the lives of others and say that they are preferable to ours. However, this is to set up false idols and lose out on the grace that could be ours.

On days when I feel hemmed in or frustrated by a way of life that is not as I want it to be, I turn to the words of Habakkuk, the Old Testament prophet. His small book is one of destruction and woes in the first two-thirds. But then something changes, as Habakkuk sees God breaking through barriers and overriding boundaries and undoing the accepted ways. And this sight is so sufficient that Habakkuk can say,

> Although the fig-tree does not burgeon, the vines bear no fruit, the olive crop fails, the orchards yield no food, the fold is bereft of its flock and there are no cattle in the stalls, yet I will exult in the Lord and rejoice in the God of my deliverance. The Lord God is my strength, who makes my feet nimble as a hind's and sets me to range the heights.[12]

As you survey the walls in your life, you might pick out the one that denies you what you most want. Then, as you read Habakkuk's words, you can insert a line in the first section:

> ". . . and although _____, yet will I exult in the Lord and rejoice in the God of my deliverance."

14

THE HOUSE IN THE FOREST

The seventh day is a palace in time which we build. It is made of soul, of joy and reticence. In its atmosphere, a discipline is a reminder of adjacency to eternity.

Abraham Joshua Heschel

A barrow-woman, blessed be God and our good laws, is as much her own mistress on Sundays as a duchess.

Hannah More

Near the old city of Jerusalem was an elegant edifice called the House of the Forest. After Solomon built the House of the Lord, he continued construction as he built his own dwelling, the House of Judgment, and a house for Pharaoh's daughter. Among these buildings was the House of the Forest, so called because it was paneled with cedar from the Forest of Lebanon. In this house, Solomon placed two hundred shields of beaten gold, three hundred bucklers of beaten gold, and a throne of ivory overlaid with fine gold, with a calf at the back and a lion standing on either side and twelve lions on the six steps approaching the throne.

But what was the House of the Forest for? If it had been just for storage of arms, there would have been no point in making it so grand. I think the House of the Forest was a symbol of leisure, of rest, of beauty and imagination. It had no specific use that historians know of, and yet it became an object of astonishment in its useless beauty. It was lined with cedar; its fragrance spoke of the forest. In housing the fruit of Solomon's imagination and his wealth, it was a visible reminder of the blessing of God upon this man who sought wisdom above riches and fame.

The House of the Forest was a place for wonder and admiration and appreciation. It was a place for interrupting the duties of the day and week and thinking about the lush forests from which the cedar was cut, and the trade from faraway nations, and the tribute of the kings and governors of Arabia which yielded the gold that was made into shields and bucklers. It was a place for remembering that Solomon's father called the God of Israel a shield and buckler.

Sabbath and Ritual

The House of the Forest was something like the Sabbath in its purpose. For the Sabbath too was carved out of time and labor for creative leisure, for worship, for appreciation, for imaginative remembering of the works of God. Rabbi Abraham Joshua Heschel calls the Sabbath "a palace in time which we build."

> The meaning of the Sabbath is to celebrate time rather than space. Six days a week we live under the tyranny of things of space; on the Sabbath we try to become attuned to holiness in time. It is a day on which we are called upon to share in what is eternal in time, to turn from the results of creation to the mystery of creation, from the world of creation to the creation of the world.[1]

He calls Jewish ritual the "architecture of time. . . . The main themes of faith lie in the realm of time. . . . The Sabbaths are our great cathedrals."[2]

On four occasions, I have invited someone from a Hebrew Christian congregation to come and lead a seder in my home. In the early part of the liturgy, before the meal, the host elevates the plate containing the three matzohs and everyone at the table touches the plate and says,

> This is the bread of affliction which our ancestors ate in the

land of Egypt; let all those who are hungry, enter and eat thereof; and all who are in distress, come and celebrate the Passover. At present we celebrate it here, but next year we hope to celebrate it in the Land of Israel. This year we are servants here, but next year we hope to be freemen in the Land of Israel.[3]

It is a gift of leisure to be able through all generations to say, "Next year . . . "

On the plate that is elevated, the middle of the three matzohs is then broken and half of it hidden to be found later by the younger children at the table, and eaten after the meal. It was this hidden half which Christ took after His last supper with His disciples and broke and said of it, "This is My body"—this middle one—"broken for you." This one which was hidden and found signifies to Hebrew Christians the burial and resurrection of Christ. This one which is discovered by young children and by those with hearts as trusting as children. This is not the talk of mortar and bricks but of leisure and time and a far country.

In His institution of the Sabbath, God gave the gift of reflection, of worship, of time, and permission to train our attention on something other than the visible world. He gave the more-than-enough principle, so that the people of God would know they need never be impoverished. They always had more than enough, for they had one day on which they did not work. A day to concentrate on eternal origins and meanings, a day for relationships, a day for contemplation and celebration together, a day for remembering who they were, whose they were, and where they had come from. A day for remembering where they were headed.

Leisure and Listening

We too need a House in the Forest, not only for regular attendance at church, but for an attitude of quiet reflection, of leaving the pursuits of the week, of feeling a permission to contemplate the holy and the wonderful. We need to feel that it is all right to take time to search out the right color and shape, the exact word or tone to express what is inside of us.

We need to feel quiet about doing nothing, just sitting and

thinking and reflecting on the meaning of being human and of possessing the possibility to know the One who made us. We need to know that it is okay to listen to the deep places in ourselves and know that God will meet us there, in the inner regions where Jesus said the kingdom of God is.

For we will never hear the word we crave, will never find the right color or form, if we are not quiet long enough for these other languages to communicate with us. We want agreement between God's world and ours, between God's love and our need, but we can't feel these without that quiet leisure which stills us in expectancy for the word about ourselves we can almost hear but cannot say by ourselves. The sentence that parses so well, as of course it will, for it is said by Him who made all words, who gave us need and will to articulate what life is about. The sentence of my life and yours is spoken by the Word Himself, and it is right.

I have only one complaint about His words—He speaks them so slowly. Years it takes sometimes to finish one sentence. And yet the words that come to us in the Sabbath silences, which can be part of any day, reach back to beginnings and forward to beginnings, and they encircle life with holy reverberations. The right words about us can be said only by the One who went to the ultimate lengths for the privilege of naming you and me as His friends, only by Him who was willing to be pierced even to death that we might hear His word of life, that word which pierces to the inmost place of our being, the place no one can see or touch or even name accurately, the place where the table of inwardness is set even in the presence of our enemies, and where we can feast with the One who sees and knows and always says the right words, "Come, for all is now ready."

I am very conscious of the blessing of physical hearing, since mine is seriously impaired, a hereditary weakness of the auditory nerves. I have sought God's healing and still believe that He can strengthen with one touch the nerves that are weak. But I would never trade even for normal hearing the goodness I have gained in learning of the silent Word, of listening within to words heard deeply in the soul, words that defy human sense at times, and yet make so much sense in terms of how God made us.

I say I have learned, and yet I have to be reminded again and again that I will not hear God's deep words if I do not settle down and be quiet, if I do not respect the Sabbath principle. If I am forever running as if the world depends on my energy or cleverness, I will not hear Him.

Dreams and Prayer

We see our most personal dreams and visions in our times of leisure, as we know deeply who we are and who we can become. When we bring our astonishing dreams into God's presence, in prayer, we often begin to know what to make of them, and get an inkling of what they will make of us. We bring them into subjection to the will of God and the Word of God as they are worked out in our experience. "Prayer is an invitation to God to intervene in our lives, to let His will prevail in our affairs; it is the opening of a window to Him in our will, an effort to make Him the Lord of our soul."[4]

In his book, *Arctic Dreams*, Barry Lopez wrote, "In individual dreams is the hope that one's own life will not have been lived for nothing. . . . You are able to stake your life . . . in what you dream."[5]

Dreams need management, and there is no better way to manage them than by prayer. We dream of what has never been done and then pull back because it has not been tried. Yet in our times of prayerful dreaming, we can come to know if the dream is something we can do. There is no law against newness. No prohibition against imagination. No tangible barrier to Catherine and William Booth reaching out to the poor in the effort that became the Salvation Army. There were no laws against Robert Raikes beginning Sunday Schools for poor children, or for Hannah More to leave her literary forms and begin to write her cheap tracts, which are credited with keeping the French Revolution from spreading to England's masses. No rule kept Dolly Cameron from rescuing countless Oriental children from lives of prostitution.

Our dreams lead us to visualize what we can do and then to plan the process of doing it. God gives new ideas, for He is the One who makes all things new, even in the living out of dreams that have taken shape in the prayerful quietness of our leisure.

Leisure and Imagination

Leisure and imagination have much to do with the world between Sundays. It is through imagination that we visualize the mirror in which we are transfigured into the likeness of the Lord, from splendor to splendor.

It is through the eye of the mind that we understand the hundreds of metaphors in Scripture. We hear, "I am the Light of the World," but we also see. We hear, "I am the Vine, the Good Shepherd, the Bread of Life, the Gate," and we see in our imaginings the meanings of the metaphors. We read the parables of Jesus and draw pictures in our minds and so understand the kingdom of God.

Those who discount the human need to visualize have no way to understand Jesus' words, "You must be born again" or "This is My body broken for you, this is My blood shed for you" or "I will give you a spring of water welling up to everlasting life." In their fear of imagination and memory and the inner recesses of personality, such people seem to want to strip the Word of God of everything but certain propositions of which they approve. The Prophet Isaiah would find himself edited to a mere shell. Jeremiah would weep over what would be lost from his lament, were such people to take a hand to his book. David would no longer be the Sweet Singer of Israel. And Jesus? Well, He would lose all His parables, His homey statements like "You are the salt of the earth" or "Take the beam out of your own eye."

It is in the leisure of imagination that we see the righteous people as trees planted by rivers of water, that we hear the turtledove coo in our land, the sea roar, the rivers clap their hands, and the hills sing aloud together before the Lord.

It is in the leisure of imaginative visualization that we watch the mountains skip like rams and hills like young sheep. That we know God rides on the wings of the wind and calls the clouds to be His chariot.

It is in such leisure that we envision a leader as the light of morning, as sunrise, a morning that is cloudless after rain.

It is foolish to deny the faculty of visualization. We can no more live without it than we can live without breathing. And why would anyone want to?

3

PURPOSE

15

SETTING YOUR OWN AGENDA

Our commitment to the transcendent is the refusal to allow the best years of our lives to happen without us. Prayer is how that refusal occurs daily.

James Carroll

The woman alone has unusual freedom to set her own agenda, to build her life, to change her pace in ways that are impossible within a family structure.

This freedom may have been one of my fascinations, as a child, about Mary Poppins. She could do things that any of us with a little luck *should* be able to do—she could fly, she drank tea sitting next to the ceiling, she conversed with animals, she made time do her bidding, she closed the gaps between now and then. She dealt with the world as a unified whole and acted as if it were all intelligible and available.

She decided when she would work, and where. She determined the agenda for any given day, and in harmony with the real needs of people. She took her young charges, Michael and Jane, into palaces in time where the moments and the hours didn't follow in the same progression as they did for earthbound people. She carved out places of rest in a weary world, so that she was continually refreshed.

Today's woman alone can come and go very much as she chooses. She can decide when and where she will eat. She can cook as much or as little as she pleases.

REFLECTIONS FOR WOMEN ALONE

She can decide where she will work and live, especially if no one else must be considered in her choice. Mothers with dependent children will want to give the needs and interests of their children high priority. However, a geographical move is not necessarily out of the question for a single mother.

A woman alone is free to invest her money as she sees best. She is able to spend her money as she wishes, to buy clothing or an addition to a collection or tickets for concerts or plays. She is free to vacation when and where she wants.

She is free to change her lifestyle. An older Christian widow who has a strong commitment to a pro-life position takes pregnant girls into her home for many months, seeing them through the births of their babies, and then helping them adjust to life afterward.

A never-married woman is a professor in a graduate school of a Christian college. As part of her work, she travels frequently in the United States and abroad. When she is at home, she attends a Spanish church in Chicago.

In my daughter's neighborhood is a woman who works part-time for a sheriff's department. Her primary occupation is to provide foster care for several children, all of whom are physically disabled.

Manipulating Time

Beyond deciding to fill our days and hours with meaningful activity, we also can decide to circumvent time as we usually experience it. Or we can extend time to be a place in which we rest. Years ago, I spent three days on a ferry bound for Alaska, seventy-two hours that became an exercise in extended time. There was nowhere to go, nothing usual to do, no activities planned, no communication with the outside world. The weather outside was unpleasant most of the way, and time passed as slowly as I have ever known it to do.

Once in a while I go to a retreat house for a day or two of quiet and change. This also is extended time, and offers a kind of rest that is hard to find in our usual schedules. When we package time in different ways, we are demonstrating that we want it to serve us, instead of our serving time.

When the woman alone refuses to manipulate time for her own good, we may wonder if she is a liege to the ought, a

servant of tradition, a subject of the commonplace, in bond-
age to boredom, or if she is opposed to taking her moments in
hand to make them serve her own purposes and God's meanings for her life.

When the Red Queen and Alice talked about the flexibility
of time, Alice said, "In our country, there's only one day at a
time."

The Red Queen replied, "That's a poor thin way of doing
things. Now here, we must have days and nights two or three
at a time, and sometimes in the winter we take as many as
five nights together—for warmth, you know."

"Are five nights warmer than one night, then?" Alice
ventured to ask.

"Five times as warm, of course."[1]

Playing with Time

"Mankind has revealed a potent, pressing desire to play with
time, to make more of it than nature has made."[2]

Just think what we do with time. We mark time, make
time, spend time, hoard time, measure time, lose time, and
gain time. We find time and make up time and waste time
and manage time and fritter away time. We redeem the time
and buy up the time. We keep time and fill time. We stretch
time and kill time.

We say that time flies or drags, stands still, escapes or
marches on. We even say that time heals.

We have time clocks, time cards, time bombs, timetables,
time machines, time traps, and time management. We speak
of small and big time, fast and slow time, overtime and
borrowed time, flying time and driving time.

We want other people to be on time and we want to be
masters of our own time. We say things are well-timed or ill-
timed, time-battered, time-consecrated, time-consuming, or
time-sanctioned.

We can go against or be with the times. We think of some
things as timely, others as timeless.

We all offer our private commentaries on time and say
along with Shakespeare,

> The time is out of joint; O cursed spite,
> That ever I was born to set it right.[3]

Reducing Time

In *The Discoverers*, Daniel Boorstin tells how man moved to ever smaller units of time, beginning with the two divisions of day and night, but continually discovering new ways for determining time that were not dependent on the sun's shadow. Over the centuries, time segments decreased in length, moving from day and night to quarter days, to hours to quarter hours, to minutes to seconds, and finally to portions of a second. During the fourteenth century, the equal hour was established. Boorstin called this achievement "man's declaration of independence from the sun, new proof of his mastery over himself and his surroundings. Only later would it be revealed that he had accomplished this mastery by putting himself under the dominion of a machine with imperious demands all its own."[4]

One day when talking with a friend, I asked what he had been doing lately, on some time off. He said, "Nothing. I do that quite well." Yet if we let it, time crowds and pushes and pinches. Most of us need help in our strategy to keep time flowing instead of flooding. There is something about the calendar God ordered for the Hebrew people that helps to keep time in order. They had regular Sabbaths, religious feasts, periods of change and celebration that put the people into a different mode of experiencing time. And I have wondered if our experience of time would change dramatically if we would build our year around festivals of celebration. For just as the Sabbath was made for people, so was time. We were not intended to become its victims.

The time pressure tends to carry over into what should be rest periods, into Sundays and vacations. We have deadlines hanging over us and see some hours on a Sunday when we could get ahead of the game a little. Especially when the work is in some way religious, we excuse our doing it on the Lord's Day by saying that it is "necessary." I have come to believe that any job that produces pressure, that causes stress, that is crowding us, is the very job we should stay away from on Sunday.

Many of us have majored in keeping away from jobs on Sunday that *look* like work and have moved instead toward activity that appears sedentary. This is a false definition of work, especially in our information age, where less and less work *looks* like work of the past. Anything regular which hangs over me, that must be done, is work of high priority for me. And this should not be done on Sunday. If it is truly worth doing, the job will get done some other time. And I will experience a day of freedom and rest, and also of knowing that my priorities are beginning to line up with God's.

We all need time with nothing to do. And yet, some people feel guilty about such inactivity, and try to treat time as if it were nothing more than a succession of minutes. But our relationship to time is not that simplistic. We have mental and biological and emotional time clocks. We need rhythm and balance and harmony in our schedules.

Today so many people are pushing themselves nearly to the limit in their race to beat the clock. While they may maintain their quality of performance for a time, they will falter eventually, as body and brain demand downtime.

Time is not going to adjust itself to our demands, for it is a created servant of people, a gift and resource, a constantly renewed object of God's creative act.

If we believe that Christ fills all, and holds all together by the Word of His power, then we must necessarily include time in the all. We need to bring God into our thinking about how best to live in time. For someday we shall go onto God's time standard and have to explain what we did with His gift to us.

I believe that part of our answer rests in what we learn about timelessness and leisure. It is after we have experienced the meaning of the Sabbath that we can adequately plan the six days between. It is when we know something of the meaning of leisure that we can invest work with its true significance. It is when we give space to our dreams that the more pragmatic realities of life find their right places in our agendas.

There are three points in existence that are timeless—before time, after time, and our perception of this moment and its need. There is a cord that passes through these three to pull them together into one moment. That cord is called Grace. And the good news is that Grace extends to the weekly calendar just as much as it does to our souls. Grace extends to the household and to the workplace, bearing its moments of timelessness and peace so that we reenter our worlds refreshed.

Restoring the Years

For some women, dealing with moments and hours is less of a problem than watching long years disappear without a suggestion of fulfillment of their fondest hopes and dreams. Most things take too long. There are mysteries in life, and we who want everything solved before the ten o'clock news is over are impatient. There are events that cause us to wonder, because they don't fit the trivia mentality of the day.

If we try to do away with those aspects of life that involve mystery and long lines of continuity and that demand waiting and wondering and, at times, wandering, we only work against ourselves. We end up impatient, bored, angry, feeling a sense of loss that is hard to identify. We look in the mirror and see only part of a person but don't know which part.

If you have had a long hope that is late in being fulfilled, if you sense that you are on a journey, that there is something ahead for you which may take considerable time, don't give up. Don't be ashamed of the long hope, especially if you think it was given to you by God. In the Bible we read of people who waited ever so long for a promise to be fulfilled. They were not idle in the meantime, but were faithful, trusting God even if He should not bring to pass what they hoped for.

Some women have been ravaged by years of pain and illness, by tragedy and loss that have more than taken their toll. When I experienced this, I thought often of the phrase, "restore the years which the locust have eaten," from the Prophet Joel. The way it is usually worded, we might think that it is a prayer. However, the text shows that God is speaking, saying that He will restore the years eaten by the plagues which He sent.

Life is complex, and all the more so because it takes place on a moving tread we call Time. We are confronted not only by the accidents of life but also by the compounded interest on choices we have made. We meet circumstances that result from sin and evil in the world, as well as those that bless and enrich our lives. We deal with our infirmities at the same time we are trying to use our giftedness. We need moments when time stands still and grace surrounds us with acceptance sung in timeless harmonies. Such commitment to the transcendent is our refusal "to allow the best years of our lives to happen without us."

16

THE CALLING

Somebody placed the shuttle in your hands,
somebody who had already arranged the threads.

Dag Hammarskjöld

God who has laid the burden on me will enable me to bear it
until He shows me how to unpack and disperse it.

George MacDonald

In recent years we have heard a great deal of discussion about
the subject of ordination for women. However, it seems to me
that there are some prior questions to be asked before consider-
ation of ordination.

Does God call women to specific works?

If so, does He call women to works that men do also?

Does God call women to works, the following of which will
put them into a difficult position with much of the religious
community?

Regardless of how we answer the questions, the fact is that
women throughout history have claimed and believed that God
called them to specific works for Him. They have believed this
so strongly that they have stood against family and clergy, have
persisted with determination that should have won medals for
courage. Some of them were downright zany, like Carrie Nation
in her temperance crusade. Eccentric as she was, she did
mobilize thousands of women and accomplished much that

never could have happened through milder, more couth methods. It would be hard to know how much to credit God for the results; fortunately, we don't have to decide the percentages.

Some women were mystical in their perceptions of God's leading, such as Mariana de Jesus of Quito, Ecuador, who was credited with saving the city from a plague. Or like Joan of Arc, who was driven to obey the Voice she heard because she believed it was the voice of God.

The woman of today who feels called by God can learn much from heroic women of the past. However, she is not much helped in knowing what to do with her sense of call in her place in time. For a call does need to be worked out in a particular setting. It is not disembodied, but takes form through the energies of a woman relating to her society. If most of the people in her world don't even consider the possibility that God could call a woman to a special work, she is confronted with some difficult questions.

What is she going to do with this persistent voice that keeps after her? This continual reminder of what she feels she should do, this persuasion that often doesn't make much sense in the context of her family or church experience? Where can she go for guidance? Or should she even try for a resolution? Is a life of following the nebulous call just too impossible even to consider?

Who Defines Women?

We said that we need to go behind the ordination question to ask if women are indeed called by God. Let's go one step behind that, and ask yet another question: who defines what a woman is and does?

We like to think we are free to be and do what we like, but for most of us, that just isn't true. We live within communities that do much of our defining for us. And we find it more comfortable to stay within those proscriptions than to break away. We all live with unwritten assumptions about what women do and don't do, say and don't say. Women who step out of line soon find that life may be more tolerable if they find another community in which to express themselves.

I find it uncomfortable to admit that women have long allowed men to define them, until I look the other direction and realize that many men permit the women in their lives to define them. Letting someone else define you is a weak thing to do, and is bound to produce anger sooner or later. I consider this cross-definition one of the primary reasons for the anger of many women toward men. And I would also credit it as the reason for years of bottled-up anger on the part of many men that often explodes in a time we call mid-life.

There has been and is discussion and dissension in the church over ordination and ministry for women. But years ago, there was similar discussion and dissension over education for women, the vote for women, their right to enter the medical profession, and on and on.

How much of the objection to women in ministry is theological and how much is purely cultural? I know that the answer varies widely group to group; but I suspect that many of those who claim to have theological objections aren't as purist as they think. No one with a theological objection to women in ministry could countenance a woman missionary going alone to evangelize the heathen, and yet this is precisely what has happened in so many fields of the world. Out of sight, these courageous women were free to do anything they wanted. They just couldn't do it around the men.

Let's take our supposing one step further. Suppose that no one ever were to be ordained. Suppose that ministry were left entirely to the obvious calling and gifting of God in a person's life. What then could a woman do?

When a woman has felt the hand of God upon her, when she feels a basic gifting for service, should she then in faith go on to prepare herself, trusting that God will make a place for her, above the objections of those around her?

We don't have to look as far as the animal world to find territorial creatures. People are highly territorial, and those in power always want to maintain their territory. No one likes his space threatened by others. Not men. Not women.

The possibility of women in ministry is a threat to the territory of men. And what is so sad about the fussing and discussing that goes on and on is that there is so much work to be done in and through the church, so much that women are uniquely gifted to do—and could easily do, starting tomorrow—if the powers that be only gave them some space and encouragement. So much that needs doing, and yet we fume and fuss about something called ordination, and leave the work with people undone. There are dozens of jobs in or through the church that women could do that would never raise the question of ordination. And yet, these areas of service usually go unfilled. It is easier to fight about protection of turf.

Of course, the good news for a woman who has heard the call of God is that God is not restricted by regulations. God always has another idea, a better plan. For many women of the past, as well as for women of today, this means that He extends His call over a long period of time, until a woman becomes so strong and so determined that no one can stop her. It may also mean that God holds her back until a time when what she can do is so necessary to a large number of people that there is just no point in others resisting her any longer. And God has His way.

When women allow men to define them, when women refuse to take seriously what they are and can become, the results are disastrous. For the married woman, the results are often less obvious, as she basks in the borrowed glory of her husband. But for the woman alone, there is no reflected glory. What she is is what she has.

The woman alone has much greater freedom to become, in directions that could be very difficult for many married women. She has more personal discretion over her time and money and location. She is not living in a day-by-day situation of mutual submission to another as in a marriage. Her energies can more freely be poured into a work.

Yet, a woman alone has certain obstacles in her way if her primary goal is to be like other women. Rather than employing the freedom in her lifestyle for good, she may be using it to conform, to feel acceptable. Rather than viewing singleness as a resource, she may see it as a trap. If this is so, she will not be responsive to the voice of God.

Florence

Florence Nightingale was one woman who believed that she had heard a call from God. As a child she thought there must be something wrong with her, because she felt life around her so pointless. And then on February 7, 1838, "God spoke to me and called me to His service."[1]

Florence felt confident that God would speak again soon and

tell her exactly what to do. However, this did not happen. In the following years, she encountered alternatives to pursuing the call: marriage to some highly eligible men, becoming a religious recluse, entering high society.

As she struggled with her sense of call from God and with the opposition she received from her family, she wrote down some of her feelings. In 1842, at age twenty-two, she wrote, "My mind is absorbed with the idea of the sufferings of man; it besets me behind and before. . . . All that the poets sing of the glories of the world seem to me untrue. All the people I see are eaten up with care or poverty or disease."[2]

In 1845, she wrote, "God has something for me to do for Him."

In 1850, "My God, I don't know myself. I cannot understand myself—how can I hope to make anyone else understand my case?"

In 1851, "My God, what am I to do. . . . Thou hast been teaching me all these thirty-one years what I am to do. . . . Where is the lesson? Let me read it. Oh, where, where is it?"

Again in 1851, "O God, what am I?"[3]

During these years, Florence was training herself in nursing, over the objections of her family, so that when there was a specific need, she was ready. In 1853, she was appointed superintendent of the Institution for the Care of Sick Gentle-women, in London.

In 1854, she volunteered to go to Constantinople and take three nurses with her to help soldiers in the Crimean War. Instead of this rather modest role, she was asked by Sidney Herbert to take "complete charge of the nursing in the military hospitals in Turkey (i.e. at Scutari). The party left England on October 21, 1854 and entered the Barrack Hospital at Scutari on November 5."[4]

By May 1855, nursing the sick had already become a second-ary interest to Florence, for now her prime concern was the welfare of the British Army. On March 16, 1856, she became General Superintendent of the Female Nursing Establishment of the Military Hospitals of the Army.

From her return to England in 1857 until her death in 1910, Florence lived as a semi-invalid. It was never proven that there was anything wrong with her. But her "neurasthenia" provided her with the time and privacy in which to continue her work. One doctor advised her, "Never get up again," and she virtually never did.

Commenting on this, Elizabeth Longford, author of *Eminent Victorian Women*, said, "Why should she? She had achieved what her 'psyche' needed: freedom from anyone who agitated her . . . a band of slave companions . . . and a stream of the great and powerful from Whitehall. . . . She saw no one . . . except by appointment. Her business was to 'advise, to encourge and to warn'—the Royal Prerogative, no less."[5]

Eccentric and difficult, she was also single-minded and dedicated, highly gifted and qualified, and she accomplished what no woman had ever before and few have since.

What Do You Do with a Call?

If you have sensed the call of God on your life, what should you do about it? Two responses are equally inadequate—to make a call a basis for contention, or to ignore the call and hope that life will just go on.

If it is God you are dealing with, you need to respond in ways appropriate to what He is asking of you. This may mean training. It should mean finding a person or a group that can understand and advise you. For somewhere along the line, the call of God should become evident to others, in the spiritual gifts He is bestowing on you.

If you feel called by God to a work you as yet can't define, you are also called to great faith and persistence, to walking on in the dark and believing that God will show His ways to you at the right time. It means doing those things that He brings to your awareness along the way; little things they may seem, but all will come together at the right time.

Living with a call means exercising patience greater than you have previously known. It means immersing yourself in the Word of God. It means asking God to define you and your expressions. It means holding rather loosely to present positions, knowing that there is something ahead for you that is probably different. But it also means doing your best in whatever work is yours right now.

It means knowing that God is greater than His people,

greater than the institutions that speak in His name, greater than your advisors. It means at times keeping your own counsel, and finding out for yourself what the Word of God says, especially when you sense conflict in the Christian community.

Unfortunately, when you start to collect words of guidance from renowned speakers and teachers on any given subject, all you discover is that they disagree with one another. This does tend to throw you back very much on the Word of God and on the Spirit of God as your teacher. But this means also a caution against becoming too private in your interpretations of the Scriptures. No course that you follow or opinion that you hold should go against the principles you find throughout Scripture, or the meaning of God's redemptive work with His people. Nor should it contradict the historic creeds of the church.

Living with a call often means living with loneliness. When Florence Nightingale was in nurses' training in Dusseldorf, she wrote to her mother, "I should be as happy here as the day is long, if I could hope that I had your smile, your blessing, your sympathy upon it."[6] A woman who strikes out in a different direction is asking for some misunderstanding.

Living with a call means exercising great faith in the goodness of God. The young Catherine Mumford had already sensed the call of God on her life before she married William Booth. Prior to their marriage, he had asked that she relinquish any place of ministry, and she told him she would never marry him under those conditions. He accepted the stipulations she placed on their marriage agreement, and later gave her far greater place in the work of The Salvation Army which they founded, as he discovered the gifts she had received from God. Writing about the matter of a call, Catherine said,

Whatever the particular call is, the particular sacrifice God asks you to make, the particular cross He wishes you to embrace, whatever the particular path He wants you to tread, will you rise up and say in your heart, "Yes, Lord, I accept it; I submit, I yield, I pledge myself to walk in that path, and to follow that Voice and to trust Thee with the consequences"?

"Oh," but you say, "I don't know what He will want next." No, we none of us know that, but we know we shall be safe in His hands.[7]

17

POSSESSING THE POSSIBLE

Our sanctification depends not on changing our works, but in doing that for Jesus' sake which commonly we do for our own.

Brother Lawrence

Holy shoddy is still shoddy.

Elton Trueblood

Women are more honest than men about nearly everything because they are more confident that no one will pay attention to their opinions. Men, trained in the male attributes of deceit and bluff, are too competitive to speak the truth about most things.

Bill Granger

I was working that week in April, representing my company at a conference in California, when I was reminded of some of the problems women face as they try to work with men.

During an evening meal, the director announced that any conferees interested in talking about women's ministries could meet together for breakfast the next morning. In the group were two pastors' wives and a consultant to women's ministries. All of the ten women were involved in their churches.

The pastors' wives were enjoying fulfilling ministries. Most of the others expressed gradations of frustration that began to focus on the familiar "them." The men who wouldn't support what the women were trying to do. The men who wouldn't let them have enough space and money and time. Them. Some of the comments I heard were:

"We are not supposed to rock the boat."

"The needs of women under forty are not being met."

"Sometimes you just have to go ahead. Don't ask anyone."

"To most men, things that women do don't matter. They figure it will all go to gossip sooner or later anyway."

"Women don't know where they fit."

"Women have limited freedom to minister, to use their spiritual gifts."

"Women are hearing two extremely different messages—liberation and submission. They are confused."

"So many women have feelings of low self-worth."

"Older women are threatened by younger women."

"Men are threatened by women."

"So many men just want to keep the women busy and out of their hair."

These comments say something not only about church work, but also about how many women feel in other work environments. As I have thought about the conference conversations since that time, I have come to realize that much more is involved than Them. The conference women and so many more are up against a whole world of Thems—our history and social mores and family traditions and religious training and education and the search for personal comfort.

A World of Difference

We live in an unprecedented time. Never in history has there been the expectation for so many unrelated men and women to work together. In times past, kinfolk worked in the home, in cottage industries, or on the farm. When a woman was queen, she worked with men—or they for her. The abbots and abbesses of the monastic system had unusual freedom to work with another.

Even in our century, most work for pay has been a man's domain until rather recently. Today about half of American women are in the work force. This calls for monumental adjustment, not only for the women, but also for the men.

In this world of unrelated men and women in the work place,

there are no binding loyalties, as in the family labors of a century and more ago. There are few checks and balances, few loves, few group traditions that temper personal ambitions in conflict.

The only checks are within individuals and from impersonal laws. But we feel no loyalty to those laws and regulations, and often little to the people we work with. And so the work place can be very impersonal.

Work is a highly formative endeavor, partly because we spend more waking hours at work than at any other activity. We spend more time with the people on the job than with any other group. We learn to think in ways that are compatible with our work. Very often our values are influenced by our employment. We tend to associate with the kinds of people we meet on the job.

For some women alone, work is the primary place where they are accepted for who they are and what they can do. It is the one place they can use their abilities, where they are not placed in an inferior position to married women. Work may be the place where they most often are affirmed as persons. It may be the only place where they regularly talk with men.

As good as it is in some respects, work is a setting that often seems alien to women. It has been run by men and for men for so long that most people don't even ask how it would be different if it were based somewhat or entirely on women's needs and skills and assumptions.

Women have learned to work in a set of relationships that assume that men will get the better shake. That men will usually be in charge. That men will be listened to more than women. While this is not always the case any more, it is still the prevailing assumption.

Recent tests reported on in *Psychology Today* and other periodicals show that in the schoolroom boys are regularly receiving more attention from teachers than girls are. One of these studies is entitled "The American Woman 1987: A Report in Depth" and was prepared by the Women's Research and Education Institute. Some of its findings about college classrooms:

● Professors tend to make more eye contact with men than with women so that male students are more likely to feel recognized and encouraged to participate in class.

● Professors are more likely to nod and gesture and, in general, to pay attention when male students are talking.

● Professors interrupt female students more than male students, often to make remarks unrelated to what the student has been saying.

● Female students are not called upon as frequently as male students.

● Male students are called by name more often than female students.

● Women are more likely to be asked questions that require factual answers, while men are more likely to be asked analytical questions.

● Faculty are more likely to respond extensively to men's comments than to women's comments.[1]

Nothing in this report will surprise a woman in the work force today. The sad thing is that another generation is being trained in the same way.

Different Skills

One positive benefit of so many women returning to the work place is that they are regaining something many of them have so desperately needed—nurture from other women. As working partners become personal to each other's needs and hopes and ambitions, they can give a quality and quantity of caring that is hard to find in many other settings.

Workers have always known how great a strength exists in being personal to each other. It is just that we are having to relearn this skill in our world of working with strangers, often people from backgrounds very dissimilar to our own. In the 1970s, American industry faltered largely at this point—those in charge forgot about people. They forgot that they employed human beings with imagination and dreams and personal goals. They forgot about the human potential.

But then, a wondrous event! In the 1980s, management rediscovered the individual. Business journals regularly carry articles on employee participation in decision making, on employee knowledge and wisdom. Managers are now called facilitators, motivators, even servants.

This radical shift to the personal, from the authoritative and secretive and gamesmanship approach of the 1970s, has not happened because industry cherishes the individual or has been converted to love, nor because being personal is good and right and natural. Rather, it has occurred because managing impersonally has been found to be financially unprofitable.

Now industry is in desperate need of people who can motivate, who can call forth latent hopes, who can bring alive what had almost died in the work scene—the belief that each person does matter and can make a difference. What is wanted are people who can restore confidence. Many women know how to do this. Granted, they may have to learn specific skills, but it is far easier to teach the skills to a motivator than to teach motivation to someone who does not understand people.

When you look at women who hold better-than-average jobs, you begin to see a pattern. Many of them are in positions that involve nurturing. Some of these fields have long been dominated by women, such as nursing and teaching. Women who work in areas traditionally led by men tend more to be in staff positions than in line jobs. You may find them in personnel, public relations, research, accounting, communications, as executive secretaries, or in specialty positions. They are usually in jobs that are at one remove or more from decision making.

Yes, there are a few women in high-paying managerial positions, but few enough that they are still subjects of feature articles in magazines marketed to working women. More common is the woman at the middle-management level who is allowed to make or be part of routine decisions that change nothing and garner no glory for her. When she comes close to a point of major decision, she is not surprised when the man above her steps in and takes over.

Sociologist Beth Ghiloni suggests that many women work in what she calls "soft jobs," which make up the "velvet ghetto." By this she means those jobs which relate to the public, educate, communicate, or deal with people problems.

Because their jobs involve dealing with the public, they are given more freedom and privileges than are managers in other departments. But the occupational segregation, dead-end jobs and denigration they experience as public affairs managers are characteristic of a ghetto. . . . This soft work is seen as superfluous by managers in other departments; public relations may be vital to the company, but there are no clearcut performance evaluation criteria. Public affairs managers are not viewed as contributing to the company, and are likely to be passed over for promotion into higher management.

While women are playing an increasingly important role in maintaining corporate power, they are not likely to gain corporate power as a result. . . . The corporation has found a way to utilize women while limiting their chances for advancement to the most powerful positions.[2]

Some students of business are seriously asking why women have not advanced more than they have. According to an article in *Fortune* magazine, it is not that women are incompetent, not that they have poor management skills, and not that they are less ambitious or work less hard. "A woman on the fast track is under intense pressure. Many corporate types believe that she gets much more scrutiny than a man and must work harder to succeed."

The article suggests three reasons why women have not advanced further. One is that many women have chosen staff jobs instead of line jobs. While this reflects a certain realism, it does affect chances for advancement.

A second reason is that women tend not to receive the same kind of constructive criticism as men do. When a male manager sees a male employee falling down on the job, he can take care of the matter in very direct terms. He may have a hard time dealing with a woman in the same way.

A third and probably major reason women have not advanced more can be termed male comfort. One consultant to several large companies said, "At senior management levels, competence is assumed. What you're looking for is someone who fits, someone who gets along, someone you trust. But that's subtle stuff. How does a group of men feel that a woman is going to fit? I think it is very hard."[3]

Different Values

Now and then I encounter a man who is so pro-woman as to be startling to me. In my reading for this book, I came across

141

two authors who contrast men and women in ways that are extremely favorable to women. The first is historian Page Smith, who is both professor and author. The second is Dr. Paul Tournier, Swiss psychiatrist and author. Both men take a look at the lives and environments of women in the context of history, for only then can they attempt to understand what is happening to twentieth-century women. In the late medieval period, most women had considerable freedom. This was in a time when people did not think of themselves so much as individuals as as members of groups in society.[4]

Something happened at the beginning of what we call the Renaissance that Dr. Tournier calls a choice

to the disadvantage of feeling and to the advantage of reason, to the prejudice of the body and the profit of the intellect, at the expense of the person in favor of things. Much more, a kind of repression took place: the repression of affectivity, of sensitivity, of the emotions, of tenderness, of kindness, of respect for others, of personal relationship, of mystical communion—and of woman, with whom all the terms in this list are linked by spontaneous association of ideas. Such is our modern Western world, advanced, powerful, efficient, but cold, hard, and tedious; a world in which . . . neuroses related to lack of love are multiplied; in which we have amassed a great wealth of things, while the quality of life has deteriorated. The quality of life belongs to a different order, that of feeling.[5]

In describing women as compared with men, Page Smith calls them

more open, more responsive, more religious, more giving, more practical than men; more loyal, far more the natural enhancers and celebrators of life; more passive or more capable of passivity, more elemental, more passionate. But then men are "more" a lot of other things and who is to say what is superior? . . . But masculine achievements, remarkable as they are, have almost wrecked us. In man's cruel overorganization of all life he has done a terrible violence to the human spirit and it is certainly a hopeful sign that in a confused, inchoate, and rather dangerous way we are at last beginning to realize this.[6]

Dr. Smith calls women essentially classless. He says that they possess an undividedness and are unwilling to compromise what matters. In contrast, men are elite, want to divide things, and are natural compromisers. Women are generalists where men are specialists. Women represent a harmonious whole whereas most men pursue a single passion.

Dr. Tournier believes that women have more sense of person than do men. Because of this women suffer from the impersonality of society. They possess a verbal superiority to men which they employ primarily in relationships.

"Women . . . do not aspire so much to autonomy as to a successful, stable, profound relationship; not to dependence, as is sometimes said, but to a relationship in which they will find true freedom."[7]

Dr. Tournier believes that most men do not really listen to women. And he wonders if the reason could be that the men are afraid of the questions the women are asking, beneath their conversation. He thinks that most men treat women with some contempt. "A man feels he has to reply to a question put by a man. A woman's question he can leave unanswered."[8] He doesn't feel the contempt can be explained only by pride or superior strength, but that it is bound up with frustrated desire. And woman, the eternal temptress, is eternally despised. "While contempt is related to desire, it is also allied to fear; all men are afraid of women—it is the fear of the unknown, for there is so much in the nature of women that seems mysterious to men."[9]

It is what Page Smith calls the "unutterable otherness of women which has dazzled men from the earliest time . . . something to which man yearns and which he fears."[10]

A Mission for Women
The ideal is for men and women to work together in complementary partnerships that call for the gifts of each. Working together does not mean women working for men, for that would be no change. It does not mean that the man determines and decides and ventures and the woman serves his

REFLECTIONS FOR WOMEN ALONE

thoughts and wishes. Working together assumes a recognition of the intelligence and giftedness of women. It assumes that women may know how to do certain things better than men do, and that what the women know how to do is important and needed in society. Page Smith says,

> Our culture seems to be more receptive than it has ever been before to those feminine qualities which are so at odds with a highly organized technological society—responsiveness, openness, celebration. The world needs both the "gifts" of woman and her remarkable social energies. . . . There is no solution to the "woman problem;" there are only tasks which require all the intelligence, skill, and patience that men and women together can bring to them.[11]

Dr. Tournier puts it this way: "The mission for women . . . concerns all women, each in her own place . . . the reinstatement of the primacy of persons over things. It is in public life and in the cultural sector that this primacy is disregarded most. . . . Our society, like our own hearts, puts the masculine values first: strength, success, prestige."[12]

As he thinks of this challenge for women to reinstate the primacy of persons over things, he says, "I warn you, ladies, that it will not be easy, because men have become accustomed over four centuries to making all the decisions. They are willing now to let you have a hand in their affairs, provided you stay quiet. A man does not like to receive advice from a woman, whoever she is."[13]

Dr. Tournier's word to the men is that instead of inviting women to accept male solitude, it seems "preferable to ask them to cure our solitude, to bring warmth back into our frozen world of objectivity, to give our mechanized society a soul."[14]

Such a mission can find its place where we work, whether for pay in the office or school, or for love of God and people in community and church and home.

18

THE NECESSARY WORK

If there is a meaning in life at all, then there must be a meaning in suffering. Suffering is an ineradicable part of life . . . without suffering and death, human life cannot be complete.

Viktor E. Frankl

Bless your uneasiness as a sign that there is still life in you.

Dag Hammarskjöld

There is only one thing that I dread: not to be worthy of my sufferings.

Dostoyevski

So much of our work seems urgent. How do we decide what is truly necessary? In one of the paradoxes of God's economy, the work which is most necessary is the one we never seek, but try to avoid. As inevitable as this work is, we never prepare ourselves for it, and try to act as if it can't catch up with us. For the necessary work is suffering.

Christ talked about work, when He said that both He and His Father worked. But of all the work Christ did, there was but one necessary task—to suffer and die for the sins of the world. So many times He made plain that His followers would join Him in that suffering, for there was and is no other way for a true believer.

We aren't skilled at learning this lesson. We aren't even good at reading the words in the Bible about suffering, for it seems such an unnecessary option. If it is forced upon us, we'll get through it somehow, kicking and screaming, or perhaps with silent dignity; but we certainly don't need to spend time thinking about it beforehand!

In much of what passes for American Christianity today, there doesn't seem to be any good reason to consider suffering. It is strangely out of place among those who are saved to succeed, chosen for celebrity, and redeemed for riches.

The Church today is sorely tempted to preach a "gospel" that promises happiness without pain, beauty without ugliness, life without death. This is what the culture about us constantly holds before us—pain and sweat can be eliminated by the right pills and the proper spray. Thus the Church is intimidated into feeling that its gospel of life-only-through-death is a bit second rate.[1]

The Cost of Living

Life is not a seamless garment. It is put together with bits of this and pieces of that, which are cut and shaped to fit the pattern. I am making a patchwork tablecloth with pieces of fabric left from dresses, a blouse, a brocade jacket, and some velvet, mostly in hues of blues and rose and white. When I finish sewing the patches to the large circle of white backing, I will begin feather-stitching along the seams. Then I will add some adornments—embroidery or applique—within the individual pieces.

My life is something like that patchwork cloth. It has a seamless backing, but that is lacking color or varied textures and patterns. Little by little, the pieces from this year and that relationship are being cut and shaped and sewn to the background, all coming together to produce something fine. Yet at what price? Consider the apparent waste in taking a small swatch from a larger piece, the loss of time and function as so many of the pieces are stored in an out-of-the-way place until they are needed. For a while, there is a look of formlessness, of lack of design and coherence.

I hope my cloth will be as beautiful as I intend. I hope also that my life will have the significance that God intends—though at what cost? In T.S. Eliot's phrase, "a condition of complete simplicity, costing not less than everything."[2]

If we have to suffer, it is more comforting if we can do it publicly, and with apparent good reason. To have to suffer anonymously, without apparent reason, offends us as much as the pain itself. The hurt goes on and on, and because of the nature of it, we can't get much sympathy from others. We may not even be able to talk with more than a couple of people about what is happening. And when this continues long enough, the suffering becomes as boring as it is uncomfortable. We feel robbed of a sense of person, and wonder what it is all about, and why we were chosen for the honor.

Why do people suffer? Is that the question? Or is it, Why do I suffer? Why am I not an exception to the existence of personal pain? Why didn't God or good intervene and stop the pattern for me and mine?

When nothing intervenes and we do suffer, we become angry. We fight back—and we should, for our resistance shows that we know we have meaning. We are not meant to submit to the results of falseness and evil. We cannot just opt for nonexistence. We know better than Job's wife did—and like Job, we complain. We argue. We talk too much and often don't make much sense. Yet our very protests are a way of insisting on our significance as persons. We cannot let go of the necessity of meaning something.

When we suffer, our choices are between giving in and fighting the enemy. The Christian knows it is worth fighting, because Christ is pro-resistance. He raided the bastions of evil. He robbed death of its final sting. He ultimately will heal all diseases, wipe away all tears, comfort all those who sorrow, and draw together all that He is now holding together.

For now, the Holder Together is always there. The Magnet clings as a center of life. And because we sense the pull toward the center, we know that we have meaning. A magnet pulls on objects that have its own properties. Christ as the center, the magnet, pulls on the likeness to God in us, and we feel the attraction. Jesus said, "And I, when I am lifted up from the earth, will draw everyone to Myself."[3]

Charles

Two centuries ago, there lived in England a man I have come to greatly admire. Charles Simeon has been called the founder of the evangelical Anglicans in England. Because of his thorough conversion to Christ while a student at Cambridge, Simeon could not be content with the free thinking in much of the church, and with the indifferent practice of religion around him. Yet, because he and his few believing colleagues newly ordained to the ministry were such a small minority, they suffered abuse and ostracism.

As a young man, Simeon was appointed rector of Holy Trinity Church at Cambridge.

> The parishioners, who were out of sympathy with his teaching, refused to go to hear him and locked the pew doors to keep out other worshipers. Seats had to be improvised in the aisles, which seats, on occasion, the parishioners threw out. This state of things continued for ten years.
>
> The undergraduates at Cambridge delighted in nothing more than hooting Simeon. . . . If ever a man had the "without the camp" experience of bearing reproach it was Charles Simeon in his early Cambridge days.[4]

In his later years, he received great honor from many of his colleagues, but he had to wait a long time for the tide to turn. During all those years, it was his practice to rise at four in the morning and spend four hours in prayer and devotional study of the Scripture. To a fellow preacher, Simeon wrote,

> My dear brother, we must not mind a little suffering. When I am getting through a hedge, if my head and shoulders are safely through, I can bear the pricking of my legs. Let us rejoice in the remembrance that our Holy Head has surmounted all His sufferings and triumphed over death. Let us follow Him patiently. We shall soon be partakers of His victory.[5]

A Thread of Gold

There are people who come into being so twisted that life can never be right for them. There are others for whom life ends in intense pain. To such people, life seems an enigma, and the more so for the strand of gold that runs through it and catches the sunlight. Why the thread of gold, if life is for dull hurt? Why the sunlight, if we can't rise to it? The shining seems a mockery.

The memory of the almost forgotten . . . the prescience of the future . . . are these only vapid imaginings to seduce us into dreaming in order to escape the physical realities?

Are they a path to a fountain that cannot be trusted, as Jeremiah said of God? Are they a mirage of a mountain that has been leveled? A reflection of a sun which has been shadowed? An echo of a word that must have been spoken but cannot be understood?

A subtlety of fragrance that mixes with our tears of confusion and frustration for a wholeness imaged somewhere, sometime, by an unseen hand that draws a soul, my soul, and then lets it sprawl out, end for end, with no sense of form?

How can a body do the bidding of the soul, if the soul hears no bidding? How can the soul know of the bidding except it be pulled to take shape to something recognizable? How can the soul recognize its source except it suffer and know its likeness to the God who suffers?

Is suffering then desirable? Not especially, in itself. Yet, within the pain, God, the Holder Together, tugs on the golden strand and pulls us ever closer to the center.

In our vulnerability, we feel other hands supporting us. As gentle as they are, still we feel the roughness of scars which will never be fully healed over, for the Infinite who became vulnerable once is once for always scarred.

The Infinite is recognizable only by the scars. The only mark of humanity that remains—scars—Scars and Sympathy too profound to simply say, "With sympathy,"and then go on.

The Infinite in the beginning of our time was as a word unformed, yet spoken for its necessity.

The Infinite in the middle time was incarnated to say the word of the beginning out loud.

The Incarnated Word couldn't help but be a colloquialism of the eternal Word, expressing the Infinite in finite terms. Yet, every accent and abbreviation made a mark.

People didn't mind the accents and abbreviations; they were

used to them. What they minded was the suggestion that those sounds stood for something they couldn't say, words their mouths couldn't form, realities they failed to see.

For this was the incarnated One scarred, in hands and feet, and because He has yet other words to say to us, it is necessary that those scars remain, for they are the only way we will recognize Him.

He comes to us in our finiteness, to us who see the sun shining on the thread of the Infinite and wonder what it is for.

In our scarring experiences, He touches us and shapes us, not taking away the scars, but forming us in a soul shape that resembles His own, entering our pain, to help us experience ours as He did His.

Light and Dark

When we read the Bible, we see the constant balancing of good and evil, light and dark, day and night. In Romans 7 and 8, we find a dramatic number of opposites:

death	life
sin	righteousness
despair	hope
law	grace
natural man	spiritual man
slaves	heirs
physical body	spiritual body
sufferings	splendor
bondage	freedom
condemnation	acquittal
separation	security
oldness	newness

Becoming a Christian doesn't mean that we skip all the items on the first list. The Apostle Paul still struggled with them, even as he wrote the letter to the Roman church.

The wonderful surprise is that we can live with the second list as a present reality. God is with us in the pain and darkness. They are not closed to Him, for He purposely entered all conditions that touch our lives so that He might be with us and rescue us from the evil.

In Isaiah 50 are two verses about darkness that have often been of great encouragement to me.

> Who among you fears the Lord? Who obeys the voice of His Servant? Who walks in darkness and has no light? Let him trust in the name of the Lord and rely upon his God. Look, all you who kindle a fire, who encircle yourselves with sparks: walk in the light of your fire and in the sparks you have kindled—this you shall have from My hand: you shall lie down in torment.[6]

What is faith but the difficult venture of believing when there is no light, when the darkness is not merely empty but oppressive, nearly suffocating the breath of life so necessary for believing that somewhere beyond there is an intelligible pathway, if ever so narrow, that can be reasonably followed.

Reasonably followed? But that means light and definition, and right now it is dark. And this is the tension—that we always want a confidence outside of what God is.

As Christians, we can expect that in our bleak experiences, God is with us, not giving light always, but being a presence to us. And in such times, we learn about Him and ourselves, and we are prepared for the season of healing.

> Our human wounds are most intimately connected with the suffering of God Himself. . . . To heal, then, does not primarily mean to take pains away but to reveal that our pains are part of a greater sorrow, that our experience is part of the great experience of Him who said, "But was it not ordained that the Christ should suffer and so enter into the glory of God?"[7]

19

A MATTER OF CHOICE

We can live any way we want.

People take vows of poverty, chastity, and obedience—even of silence—by choice. The thing is to stake your calling in a certain skilled and supple way, to locate the most tender and live spot and plug into that pulse. . . .

I think it would be well, and proper, and obedient, and pure, to grasp your one necessity and not let it go.

Annie Dillard

Most people get what they want if they will it enough, get what they ultimately live for, if they shape their lives to it.

Sibyl Harton

When I pray, I have to make a choice, a very fundamental choice: namely, will God be God of my life or not?

Peter G. van Breemen

The most fascinating thing about decision making is not the process we use in deciding, but the reasons and assumptions about life behind our decisions. We decide everything within a personal framework. We move in response to what is pushing and pulling us, pressuring and preventing us. We decide in deference to our dreams, our ambitions, our fears.

One reason some of us have a hard time making decisions that are good for us is that we haven't met our own standards for life. We are sitting around waiting to get lucky, waiting for our number to come up, for the man to come along, and then we will begin living. I don't know any other word for this but *gambling*. Push the right buttons, pull the right levers, put your money on the right things, and God will reward you.

Thinking clearly about decision making is difficult, because there is an element of truth in doing the right things and coming up fortunate. If we work hard, we probably are going to have more success, more money than the person who doesn't. If we live in a healthy manner, we likely are going to live longer than those who indulge in destructive habits. If we are good to other people, we probably will be happier and have more friends than the person who doesn't care about others.

But not necessarily. The story of Job is played over and over, in people who pushed all the right buttons, pulled all the right levers, and things turned out to be bad. They met with disaster. They got the incurable disease. They were deserted or betrayed. We meet wonderful, caring women who don't have husbands.

Not long ago, I met a woman who is one of the most charming and warm and interesting people I have ever known. She has never married and is filling her life with all sorts of challenging areas of work and relationship and challenge and leisure. But she wants to marry. She wants it very much, and has her eye on a certain man, who is also a good and fine person. If they don't marry, I know she will be sad, but her life won't fall apart. It is too full of other good things. She is too mature a person.

My friend is something of an exception for a woman nearing forty. For we have all seen women who in desperation marry men everyone knows they shouldn't. To watch them, you would think the institution of marriage was a social work career. The human reclamation they have in mind rarely works, but they don't find that out until it is too late. British novelist George MacDonald had something to say about this, over one hundred years ago.

Women are being constantly misled by the fancy and hopes of being the saviors of men! It is natural to goodness and innocence, but nonetheless is the error a disastrous one. It may well be that a woman does more to redeem a man by declining than by encouraging his attentions. One who obeys God will scarcely imagine herself free to lay her person in the arms and her happiness in the bosom of a man whose being is a denial of Him. God cares nothing about keeping a man respectable, yet will give His very self to make of him a true man. But that needs God; a woman is not enough for it. This cannot be God's way of saving bad men.[1]

We make choices in an unfair and uneven world. We make choices for persons we really don't understand—our selves. We make choices in a world we can't control. We make choices, and then the rules change and nothing turns out the way we thought it would.

We look at people in the Bible who made choices, and lots of times things didn't turn out well, and God didn't do anything about it. Those we read about in Hebrews 11 are lauded for their great faith and heroic ventures. We don't hear much about the frustrated hopes, the unfulfilled dreams, the suffering and fatigue and rejection. These were people who walked with God and died in faith. Most of them did not possess much of what they believed in, what they had seen afar off, and they confessed themselves no more than strangers or passing travelers on earth.

People who use such language are plainly looking for a country of their own. If their hearts had been in the country they had left, they could have found opportunity to return. Instead, we find them longing for a better country, a heavenly one. This is why God was not ashamed to be called their God; He has a city ready for them.

It is when we make choices that we find out if we too are people with an eye on the far country, people who see a king in his splendor, people who can say with the three children of Israel that God is able to deliver them, but if He doesn't, that's all right too. People who know when to stay and when to run, when to dissemble and when to confront.

Some of the people in Hebrews 11 overthrew kingdoms, established justice, saw God's promises fulfilled, quenched the fury of fire, grew powerful in war, received back their dead, went from weakness to strength. But others, just as faithful, were tortured to death, faced jeers and flogging, even fetters and prison bars, were stoned, sawn in two, put to the sword, knew great poverty and distress, were refugees in deserts and hid in caves and holes in the ground.

We don't exactly aspire to such a life. We don't sign up for hardship. We don't choose the way of suffering. Nor, I am sure, did they choose suffering for its own sake. But in the course of their faithfulness, it happened to them, and these are the people of whom God is not ashamed.

When the writer of Hebrews finishes his list, he asks, "What of us?" With all these faithful people around us like a cloud, will we now throw off every encumbrance, every sin to which we cling, and run with resolve the race in which we are entered, with our eyes fixed on Jesus, on whom faith depends from start to finish? For Jesus endured the cross and has taken His place at the right hand of the throne of God.

Jesus, who submitted to opposition from sinners, who struggled against sin, now watches as we are trained to be part of His family.

I said earlier that we make choices within a framework. For the Christian, Hebrews 11 and 12 are a suitable framework, filled with the right assumptions for life for the person who wants to live faithfully before God.

There is an old Spanish saying, "Take what you want, and pay for it." When we live with the aspirations of the chapters in Hebrews, what we want is influenced by what God values. What we want takes into account the health of our souls.

In the Old Testament, there is a story about the Children of Israel demanding something of God—meat, in this case—because they were tired of eating manna. God was weary of their complaining and gave them what they asked for, so much meat that it made them very sick. In Psalm 106, we read a commentary on this event:

They soon forgot His works; they did not wait for His counsel, but lusted exceedingly in the wilderness, and tested God in the desert. And He gave them their request, but sent leanness into their soul.[2]

This story inserts a complicating factor into the matter of choices. There was nothing wrong with meat. And at times, we want things that are perfectly all right in themselves, but which work against God's purposes for us. Thinking about this long enough could almost paralyze us into inaction, except for one emphasis I have found helpful in recent years. I believe that God honors our right intentions. If we want to seek His way, want His long purposes in our lives, I believe that He will guide us to find them.

I can't claim that He will keep us from making choices that seem wrong—because I don't know how God sees that sort of thing. I do know that He will keep us in His love, and will continually urge us on toward the good, which ultimately is Himself. I know that He will not give us leanness of soul if we want His way, but will lead us to the richness of life He wants to give to His children.

It was said of Malla Moe, "One might explain her life by irresistible grace. When you love, honor, and worship Christ, even His whisper is irresistible. That is the way God directed her life."[3]

I too can listen for His whisper and respond to His irresistible grace. I can stalk my calling. I can grasp my one necessity.

20

ENLARGING YOUR WORLD

Life refuses to reduce itself.
You were born to be significant and to count.
You are bigger than your method.

Dennis Kinlaw

After I moved into my new home in 1986, my son and son-in-law hung a large framed mirror for me in my dining room. Before, it had always been hung vertically, but this time I wanted it positioned horizontally. It fills much of the far wall and enlarges the room in its reflection.

In an analogous way, we can become mirrors of life to enlarge our worlds and to see more deeply. I was reminded of this one evening as I watched my daughter rocking her new baby to sleep, with a look of pure motherly joy on her face. I thought how some childless women would respond to her delight. This picture which is so lovely in its contentment is a reminder not only of their being unmarried but also of their lack of children. Knowing how difficult this is for some married women who are childless, I can only guess what it is for the unmarried, and I would never want to seem to simplify a dilemma that is far from simple. And yet, there must be some answer.

I think I know what the answer is not—it is not in avoiding the picture of the happiness a mother feels. It is not in bitterness, not in envy, not in the morose turning inward that sometimes happens.

We are all given the possibility of extraordinary growth in life, of reaching to understand and appreciate the experiences of others. For the woman alone, such appreciation of another's joy in marriage and motherhood is not easy. And yet, I believe it is a Christian response. This means having to deal with feelings of self-pity, of being left out of the normal flow of life. It means asking God what He wants to give to fill the empty places, for He is always desiring to do that for us. It means asking Him what we can do with our extra time and energy. It means involvement in the growth of the younger generation.

We read in the Bible that we are the way we think. A woman who spends much of her time thinking about what she doesn't have and can't do will soon feel like a sieve. Nothing will benefit her very much. Everything, no matter how lovely, will fall right through. She will feel like a person who isn't, and may think that real life is for other people.

It is true that some women have been so deeply hurt by others that they cannot by themselves put together a good life. But with the wide availability of help, they can at least reach out for assistance. They can at least find someone who will walk with them to the beginning of a good way of life.

To enlarge our lives, we have to enlarge our thoughts, our dreams, our courage. We need to be willing to risk, to fail, to try, to venture, to dare. We need to be constantly growing in mind and soul, in awareness and wisdom, so that as we come into larger places in life, we can truly occupy them.

People have varying needs for space, for mobility, for change, for ever-enlarging horizons, and for new challenges. However, even the most contented homebody needs to be learning, asking, wondering with consistency.

We all can learn new skills, can ask more significant questions about life. We can better use the inheritance we have received from our background, our ancestry. For good or bad, it is ours. In *Lake Wobegon Days*, Garrison Keillor lists his Ninety-Five Theses, his understandings of life bequeathed to him by his family. I could have written some of the same ninety-five, coming, as he did, from Norwegian parentage—on one side, anyway. Some of the "gifts" caused him grief, some a pause, and some were a strength. But all were with him as the sun is with the morning.

We are all like the householder in Jesus' parable, with a storehouse of treasures we can use as we will. However, if we see everything on our shelves as white elephants, we will feel like the manager of a pawnshop.

Part of enlarging life is getting rid of excess baggage. We can't pull everything with us. Even if life was a certain way for our parents or grandparents or neighbors, we don't have to imitate them in every particular.

Part of enlarging life is to evaluate and take hold of our abilities. We can always build on strength. We can decide what really matters. We can feed our spirits and minds. We can care for our bodies. We can regularly reassess our resources for living. We can invest our inheritance, so that we add to the emotional and spiritual wealth of the world.

Mary

I have a friend in England, Mary Skinner, whom I visited in 1985. I first met Mary in Ecuador in 1966, when she was an independent missionary, living half of the time in Quito and the other half in Puyupungu, an Indian village set at the junction of two rivers. Moving back and forth as she did between city and village meant not only an adjustment in physical surroundings but also in value systems. It meant relating to people differently and living with a flexibility that could incorporate wide contradictions.

In 1969, I spent three days with Mary in her jungle home, a frame house built up on stilts, and complete with outhouse at the end of a short path through the woods. Mary was the only white person living in the village, and came to be known affectionately as "Old Mary."

From her background in England to Puyupungu is a long distance in every way, and in her book, *If You Came to Live Here*, Mary wrote of the stretching that went on in her. She found life in Puyupungu

> hilarious, exasperating, joyful, sad, tranquil, confusing, exhausting, restful, noisy, quiet, pathetic, frightening, depressing, and rewarding. Not all at the same time, of course. Most of all, it has been a time of learning and relearning. A time of learning lessons that I had failed to learn, not been ready to

learn or not wanted to learn in England. Learning lessons that God, my Heavenly Father, wanted me to learn, and which, for the most part, my Indian neighbours have been instrumental in teaching me.[1]

I was especially impressed with chapter 2 in Mary's book, "The Gifts," because it speaks to the growth that takes place in us when we learn to give and receive within a culture quite different from the one we are accustomed to. With Mary's permission, I am including part of that chapter here, with its gifts of stones, fish, and water.

After two weeks in her Quito apartment, Mary was in a Missionary Aviation Cessna with pilot Dave Osterhus. As they circled low over the village of Puyupungu, they could see the village square with houses lining it, the trails down to the rivers and the point where the two rivers meet. And then, writes Mary,

as we made a low pass over the village itself, I could see the airstrip neat, clean and straight, surrounded by jungle.

Looking up, Octavio, Atanasio's son, paused as he climbed uphill. He straightened himself, lifted his free arm to shield his eyes from the sun. He saw the plane and thought, "That'll be Old Mary." Readjusting his fishing tackle and early morning catch on his strong, bare, brown shoulder, he continued his sure stride on the uneven trail to his home.

His stepmother, Aguasanta, heard the plane and moved from the open fire in the centre of the large room to the doorway of her thatched roofed, bamboo-walled home. Several chickens scattered as she shooed them ahead of her. She looked up.

"Old Mary's coming," she called out to her husband. Returning to the fire, she shifted a large, metal, blackened pot away from the direct flame of the burning wood, picked up an empty one, wiped its inside with her hand and hurried out of the house. Her bare feet carried her small frame with graceful ease as she quickly followed the trail down to the river from which Octavio had just come. . . .

The plane entered its final turn. The ground, rushing up, felt solid as we bumped and then gradually came to a standstill. It was always a huge relief to be safely on the ground again. I waved to my neighbours who stood on the bank by the entrance to the airstrip waiting for the propeller to stop. As I loosened my seat belt, David leaned behind me to open the door. I backed out of the plane, groping for its step with my right foot. Shifting my weight, I lifted my left foot clear of the seat and lowered myself on to the airstrip.

"Will I never discover a more graceful way of getting out of this plane?" I asked myself. Turning, I greeted my friends as they now stood around me. Touching my hand, they asked me in turn, "Are you living?"

"Yes, I'm living. And you? Are you living?" I replied.

"Yes, we're all living," they all agreed. Everyone helped unload the plane, waiting in line to receive the packages as David handed them through the opening. Everyone kept up a running commentary.

"No, that's too heavy for you. Here, Olivia, you take it."

"What's in this one, Old Mary?"

"Let me see. Looks like books. Who'll take the eggs? Careful with them."

There were numerous comments on my many packages. My neighbours seemed to manage on so little, while I needed so much for ordinary everyday living. With great good humour everything was finally placed on the other side of the airstrip's entrance. After thanking the pilot for the flight and reminding him of his next visit, I joined my neighbours who were once again standing on the bank.

"Clear?" asked the pilot. I looked around carefully.

"Clear," I answered. We waited for him to taxi to the village end of the airstrip. Once there he turned to face us. We watched him as he sped past us and lifted quickly into the air.

"He flies!" the children yelled as they jumped from the bank on to the airstrip with their arms outstretched in imitation of the plane's wings, and as they enjoyed the wind thrown back from the propeller like a giant fan.

With the plane high and clear of the trees at the far end of the airstrip, we were able to turn our attention to the packages. They needed to be taken to my house.

"Who'll take the basket of vegetables?" I asked. One willing volunteer.

"Careful how you lift it. Keep it level. On to his head now. Is that comfortable?" He assured me it was. With his example everyone offered to help. We left the airstrip by the trail that leads to the village square. As we walked single file I kept one eye on the trail and the other on my purchases being borne ahead. As I walked, I worked out in my head the right order for the chores I needed to do before dark. I would have to light the paraffin refrigerator first so that the butter, milk and meat would not spoil. Then I would light the wood-burning stove so that there would be plenty of hot water. Next I would sweep the house, make my bed, drink a most necessary cup of tea and have something to eat.

Still thinking, I arrived at the steps of my thatched-roof house; my home built up on stilts. I glanced at the space under it, where I hung my washing when it rained, and looked more closely. Something was different.

"What's happened to the holes?" I asked. A few weeks earlier I had complained that nearly all the chickens in the neighbourhood seemed to delight in spending their nights under my house, digging themselves in and the dust out.

"The holes?" I questioned again. The children giggled.

"We filled them with stones," they replied. "We thought it would make you happy." Make me happy? I was delighted. What a lovely, unexpected welcome-home present.

I walked up the steps and on to the porch, found the key to the padlock and unlocked my door. My dog was the first to enter. He plonked himself down under the dining room table, content to be allowed in after being denied the privilege during my fortnight's absence in Quito. My helpers handed me my bundles and I thanked them. When the last one had gone down the steps I began my chores. What had I decided to do first? The thing I disliked most. It is no use whatsoever getting angry with a paraffin refrigerator. Patience is the virtue most needed. I bent down and lifted the container to see if any paraffin had leaked out in my absence. . . .

Now it was time to light the wood-burning stove. I had been shown early in my jungle life that the quickest and most lasting fires are to be lit with dry paper, dry wood and dry matches. . . . I had just lit the paper when the house began to shake. An earth tremor? No, just someone running up my steps.

"Old Mary, are you living?" Recognizing the voice, I replied, "Yes, Octavio. And you and the family? Are you living?" Pointless question on my part, I concluded, as I looked at him. Octavio, a stocky, sturdy young man, full of life and energy, stood there with both hands outstretched. I took the empty one and shook it warmly. His smile widened and his brown eyes brightened as he stretched the other nearer me.

"I saw the plane," he said, "And thought you must be coming, 'She'll want some fish,' I thought, and so I've brought some. Here, take it." I looked at the gift he held out to me, took it and thanked him sincerely. First, the stones from the children, and now fish from Octavio. I found a plate, slipped the piece of fish from its banana-leaf wrapping, noted with gratitude that it had been beautifully cleaned, and put it carefully into the refrigerator. Octavio and I chatted together about his family and my trip to Quito. When we had finished talking he bounded down the steps and strode across the village square back to his home.

I resumed my housecleaning with a lighter heart. Having checked the fire and added some wood, I found a broom and started to sweep my bedroom. . . .

"Old Mary," called a woman's voice, "are you living?" I hurried to the porch to greet Aguasanta, whose name means Holy Water, as she reached the top step.

"I heard the plane and told my husband, 'That'll be Old Mary.' Then I thought, 'She'll need water'." As this elderly, sparrowlike woman said this, she handed me a large bucket, black with smoke on the outside, but heavy and full with clear, fresh water. I needed both hands to lift it from hers. I set it down and thanked her most sincerely. I was grateful. First, stones from the children, then fish from Octavio, and now water from Holy Water.

Later that day, as I enjoyed the peace and quiet with no chick-chat under the house, and ate the well-prepared fish, and drank tea made from the gift of water, I thought of the cost of the three gifts.

Stones from the beach. The children had to watch and wait for the days when the river was low for then the large, smooth stones would not be hidden. . . . Going down to the river was easy for the children. It was fun to start from the top of the trail and race down, with an empty basket tugging behind. It was the time spent on the beach, selecting the stones, lifting them and placing them in the basket, and then the return journey, with the weighted baskets resting on their backs and held in place by a carrying band across the forehead, that cost something. . . .

Fish. That was Octavio's gift. He had gone before day-break to catch that fish. He had been thinking of his wife and children as he worked in the canoe and cold water, carefully placing his nets. He was catching fish for them. So it cost something for him to give to a foreigner. . . .

Then the third gift, the water. Mark 9:41 (J.B.P.) says, "Jesus said, 'In fact I assure you that the man who gives you a mere drink of water in My name, because you are followers of Mine, will most certainly be rewarded.' " Aguasanta's gift wasn't a mere drink but a whole bucket-ful. Her gift had cost her time and energy. She had to go down to the spring, fill the bucket and carry it back uphill.

I was deeply touched and surprised by my neighbours' simple, no-strings-attached giving and the cost involved. Why should they have gone to so much trouble for some-one who does not look like them, walk like them, talk like them or smell like them? Was it because they had learned the meaning of those words of the Lord Jesus who said, "Happiness lies more in giving than in receiving"?[2]

Living with Paradoxes
Jesus said, "Ask and you shall receive." He also said, "Give and it shall be given unto you."

When we learn to do both, to give and to receive, it doesn't really matter whether the two lines continually widen or converge and cross. Either way, the road ahead is eventually enlarged for us beyond imagination.

Some people assume that the enlargement of life requires money. That is not necessarily so. There are ways to expand life without having to own all that we use. To enlarge life generally means risk, and risk means letting go of something.

For the Christian woman, a major factor in the enlargement of life is learning to live with the paradoxes of the kingdom, that the last shall be first, the poor shall be rich, that those who would be great shall serve, and that a poor woman who gave two mites gave more than all the rich of Jesus' day.

Living a larger life involves deeply knowing that God owns all things and that we use some of those things temporarily. The less property-conscious we are, the more likely we are to get our priorities straight. I am not advocating a disregard for matter, or for property. Anything in our care deserves proper attention. But our concentration should not be on the myth of owning, but on the fact of responsibly using what we have.

We can't live without money and goods and property. In the United States, women control more money then men do, often because older widows manage the estates left to them by their husbands. But many women who have never married also accumulate considerable amounts of money. One element of stewardship is the making of a will that ensures disposition of property according to the wishes of the individual. And yet, seventy percent of Americans die without a will. For the Christian, this is not responsible behavior. The good that a woman has sought to do during her life can be continued after her death. In her later years, if she so chooses, both she and her charities can benefit from her estate through annuities. But this care to what will happen later is an extension of her attitude toward money and property during her younger years

One of the deepest paradoxes in the Christian life is the existence of the cross. Not only the cross on which Jesus died, but the cross we are to build in our lives. There is no surer way to an enlarged world than to go the way of the cross. We sense the extent of our potential and reach for its fulfillment, when we do. For our gifts from God want and seek their own expression.

Yet, on our way to fulfillment, we find a cross in the way, and hear a voice, "Come to Him and die to your small ideas." God wants us to offer back to Him the gift we think is ours— our selves and our possibilities. He always has a better idea, a larger possibility than we can see. It is only when we let go that we can say to God,

I want Your full will. Give me the grace to reach out and take that which is right, no matter what the cost, because I know that on the other side of that pain there is deliverance, resurrection, freedom, release, life, and Your presence.[3]

21

THE MIRROR OF THE HOLY

Our age is characterized by . . . shallow patterns of self-rejection and self-acceptance. In both cases the self is as dry and shriveled as a prune.

Alan Jones

Prayer takes the mind out of the narrowness of self-interest and enables us to see the world in the mirror of the holy. For when we betake ourselves to the extreme opposite of the ego, we can behold a situation from the aspect of God.

Abraham Joshua Heschel

My father died in April of 1972. The next day as I sat in the pastor's study planning the funeral service, one song kept going through my mind, the only song I ever heard my unmusical father sing.

> I've reached the land of corn and wine,
> and all its riches freely mine;
> Here shines undimmed one blissful day,
> for all my night has passed away.
>
> O Beulah Land, sweet Beulah Land,
> as on thy highest mount I stand,
> I look away across the sea,
> where mansions are prepared for me,

and view the shining gloryshore,
my heaven, my home, forevermore!

Edgar Page Stites

Because the song seemed so much a part of his life, I asked two men from our church to sing it at the funeral. After the service, my father's brother, David, told me that he had a hard time maintaining his composure during that song. He said, "You know, that was our mother's working song."

My grandmother, Minnie Penzel Sanderson, had bequeathed this vision of working with another land in view to her sons, Harold and David, and now to me, and I was thankful. For I can think of no better way to live today than with the reminder that there is another day and another land.

Grandma must have known that the heavens are not locked, that the river is close by, that the loved ones already gone are still loving, and that we work not far from the city whose maker and builder is God. In her little Nazarene church, they must have read the words from Hebrews 12—right in the middle of a chapter about our attitudes and actions—"You have come to Mount Zion and to the City of the living God, the heavenly Jerusalem, to countless hosts of angels, to the festal gathering and the church of the firstborn."

Grandma must have known the closeness of the cloud of witnesses mentioned in Hebrews 12:1, and felt the gentle presence of the Saviour, and heard the songs of acceptance in Beulah Land, where no one is a stranger.

Grandma's life was primarily in the home. Mine has been in the home, school, church, mission, and office. And the reality of that other land goes with us anywhere.

But it is not merely the fact of another land and a future day that we want. What we crave is *a loving connection* between this country and that one. We want *a lighted pathway*. When we go through deep waters, when the storms threaten to undo us, we want *a line of safety*. And in all of our days, we want *a sufficient reason* for our being, in relation to His.

A Loving Connection

After years of devoted service to God, the Apostle Paul wrote, "For I am persuaded that [nothing] shall be able to separate us from the love of God which is in Christ Jesus"[1]

This loving connection is always in place from God's side of the matter. Even if we don't recognize it, the connection does us good every day of our lives, through what we call common grace, which extends to all people.

But as a loving connection between two people is richer if it is actively reciprocal, so with God. When we are open to His gifts and to His glory, when we want to know Him and to be known by Him in the inner places of our being, we can see ourselves as daughters of the heavenly King.

A Lighted Pathway

In Solomon's Proverbs is a beautiful verse that speaks of the path we walk: "The path of the just is like the shining light, that shineth more and more unto the perfect day." Another translation reads: "The road the righteous travel is like the sunrise, getting brighter and brighter until the daylight has come."[2]

This pathway puts some definition in the connection between the worlds. It is not a place to grope in total darkness, for there is always the aura of God's light, if not His brilliance, and fellowship with others going the same direction. And as surely as the dawn moves toward the daylight, so we move into ever growing light. The phrase "the perfect day" or "the daylight" can have two meanings. It can be the final day, but it also can mean any future day, in the sense of growing completeness. This is reassuring, because none of us wants to wait for heaven to enjoy life's fullness.

A Line of Safety

In an age of insecurity, the children of God are held steady by a cord of safety that is secured by an anchor. This anchor rests in a most wonderful place, in the holy of holies in heaven. The tabernacle and the temple of the Old Testament contained such a place where the high priest would enter once a year to make sacrifice for the sins of the people. This earthly holy of holies pictured such a place in heaven, where Jesus entered after He had made a perfect sacrifice for our sins.

We read in Hebrews that the hope we have in Christ is an anchor of the soul—"an anchor that can neither break nor drag.

It passes in behind the veil, where Jesus has entered as a forerunner on our behalf, having become, like Melchizedek, a high priest forever."[3]

At the time of His crucifixion, the veil of the temple tore from top to bottom, just as His flesh was torn for us. Now, the anchor of our souls which secures us is held in Jesus' flesh, His body, His substance. He who holds the worlds together is our safety.

A Sufficient Reason

We look around at the tragedies of life and think, "It makes no sense." When we see enough events that make no sense, we can be tempted to say that personal experience has no meaning. This produces conflict, for we know deep inside ourselves that we do have significance. And we want desperately that our work and our relationships shall have meaning. In a world that seems to make no sense, we hope that somehow our lives, at least, will attach themselves to a cosmic sensibility.

There is a logic in the world. Logic made the world. The Logic of God is the Logos, the Word, by which He spoke the worlds into being, and also the Word through whom He is reconciling the world to Himself.

Christ is called the Word, the Logos. As God's Word to us, He is the ultimate connection between heaven and earth. For He is the Word that makes sense of the human condition. He is the Word who can search our innerness and reach to the hidden places of our thoughts and intentions. His Spirit is the oil for lighting the lamp of our spirits, so that we can come alive to God. Christ is God's Word of reconciliation and grace through whom we may be saved. For only God, the Giver of light, the Securer of souls, can say a Word adequate to establish such connection between His world and ours.

The Speech in Your Soul

In C.S. Lewis' retelling of the story of Cupid and Psyche, *Till We Have Faces*, Orual was a woman very much alone. As the eldest daughter of the king, she heard over and over how worthless she was for not being a boy and for not being beautiful. As if his words were not enough, her father used mirrors to assure her how ugly she was. After she became queen, Orual took to wearing a veil, to hide her ugliness and to give her a protective shield behind which to live.

Orual had many complaints against the gods for the suffering and losses she had endured, the worst of which was the loss of her sister Psyche. Before she could resolve her complaints, as an old woman, she was stripped of her veil as she stood before the judge with her grievance book in hand, to say what lay deep in her heart. She read her complaint again and again until the judge stopped her and she heard for the first time her real voice, and knew that the complaint was the answer.

To have heard myself making it was to be answered. . . . When the time comes to you at which you will be forced at last to utter the speech which has lain at the center of your soul for years, which you have, all that time, idiot-like, been saying over and over, you'll not talk about joy of words. . . . Till that word can be dug out of us, why should they hear the babble that we think we mean. How can they meet us face to face till we have faces?[4]

Then Orual saw as in a dream her beautiful sister Psyche and was led by her to a pool where the god was coming to judge Orual. With each breath, she drew "new terror, joy, overpowering sweetness. I was pierced through and through with the arrows of it. I was being unmade. I was no one. . . . The earth and stars and sun, all that was or will be existed for his sake. And he was coming. The most dreadful, the most beautiful, the only dread and beauty there is, was coming. The pillars on the far side of the pool flushed with his approach. I cast down my eyes."[5]

And as she did, she saw two Psyches in the water, both beautiful beyond imagining. One of them was herself. In all the years of forgetting how she looked and giving her full attention to her people, she had become beautiful. Now Orual had her real face, as well as her real voice.

The last words she wrote in her book of complaints were, "No Answer." "I know now, Lord, why you utter no answer. you are yourself the answer. Before your face questions die away. What other answer would suffice? Only words, words, to be led out to battle against other words."[6]

Beyond the Veil

Where can we see our real faces? Where can we hear our real voices? Where can we resolve our complaints against the Almighty? Within a kind of life we need, but may resist, a life that pursues us even as we run away from it—the life of prayer in which we see into the mirror of the holy that reflects God's world of surprises and endless possibilities.

In *Crain's Chicago Business*, just before Christmas of 1986, there was an article by a professor at the Divinity School of the University of Chicago on the best way to prepare for Christmas. He contrasted our compulsion to plan our lives in detail with the unexpectedness of the coming of Christ.

> For what is the birth of this child in Bethlehem but a gentle intrusion into the world of the innkeeper's supply and demand, timely payments in the tax collector's office and the tedium of the nightshift out on the hillsides with the sheep?
>
> On this night, the routine requirements momentarily lose their power, and the initiative passes from the commanders and the kings to a baby lying in a manger.
>
> Suddenly, what is possible is not limited by our resources, or even by our imaginations. That which we can accomplish is put to use in ways we never planned and could not have anticipated. . . .
>
> So long as we remain isolated in a world defined entirely by our own plans and responsibilities, there will be little hope, because there will be little need for it. Also, there will be few surprises.
>
> But the world into which the Christ child is born is a rather different place, in which hope alone is equal to the measure of human need, and we are rescued . . . by a surprising gift that appears in an unexpected place.[7]

Opening up to hope is like taking off the veil. We become vulnerable, as we wait for something we aren't sure we want.

We want to be close to God, but we also want to keep some distance. We want real inner peace, but we also want to hold on to the excitement of the restless search.

Why this attraction and repulsion at the same time? I think that our ambivalence about prayer reveals to us what kind of

God our God is. We intuitively know that God is not someone who just seeks our occasional attention, and waits for our
occasional prayers. God is not someone who can easily do
without us. . . . If God were that kind of God, we would not
experience so many tensions when we enter in His presence
to pray. No, our tensions come from the awareness that God
is a jealous lover . . . a God who is always after us, looking
for us, and who cries out each time He finds us with a divine
despair: "Do you love Me, do you love Me, do you really
love Me?"

We are afraid that the God who says He loves us will prove
in the end to be more demanding than loving. . . . I think
our fearful hearts are saying: "Can I really trust God? Will He
really show me His love when I don't keep anything hidden
from Him—neither my own pain nor the pain of the world—
or will I be crushed by His anger and lose the little bit of
freedom I have so carefully carved out for myself?"[8]

Yet, what other way is there but to take off the veil so that we
may see God's hands reaching for us—one of grace and one of
holiness—drawing us closer to Himself and His ways. For His
holiness and grace offer our only hope of living our days as one
piece, rather than allowing our energies to be fragmented.

Holiness is not some faraway fantasy,
for the grace of God has brought it near.

Holiness says, "See what you can become."
Grace says, "Come on, I'll help you get there."

Holiness shows us the invisible door between the worlds.
Grace keeps the door open for us.

Holiness paves the pathway we take.
Grace holds the lantern for us.

Holiness prepares a perfect place for us.
Grace ties our anchor rope there.

Holiness gives sufficient reason for life.
Grace is sufficient for the unreasonableness of life.

Holiness shows us the splendor of the Lord.
Grace transfigures us into His likeness.

NOTES

CHAPTER 1

1. *Working Woman*, February 1985, p. 113.
2. ABC-TV report, February 1986.
3. Geoffrey Chaucer, *The Canterbury Tales*, Chicago: Encyclopaedia Britannica, Inc., 1984, pp. 256–277.
4. Elizabeth Longford, *Eminent Victorian Women*, New York: Alfred A. Knopf, 1981, p. 18.
5. Page Smith, *Daughters of the Promised Land*, Boston: Little, Brown and Company, 1970.
6. Rae VanDorn, "Dealing with the Dreaded," *World Christian*, September/October 1986, p. 25.
7. Veronica Zundel, "Going Spare?" *Third Way*, July 1986, pp. 22–23.

CHAPTER 2

1. Jacques Ellul, *The Humiliation of the Word*, Grand Rapids: William B. Eerdmans Publishing Company, 1985, p. 52.
2. Anthony Bloom, *Beginning to Pray*, New York: Paulist Press, 1970, p. 66.
3. Edith Deen, *Great Women of the Christian Faith*, New York: Harper and Brothers Publishers, 1959, p. 281.
4. *Ibid*. p. 280.
5. *Ibid*. p. 281.
6. *Ibid*. p. 282.
7. *Ibid*. p. 287.
8. Robert Hall Glover, *The Progress of Worldwide Missions*, New York: Harper and Brothers, 1953, p. 114.
9. *George MacDonald: An Anthology*, C.S. Lewis, Editor, New York: The Macmillan Company, 1947, p. 8.
10. 1 Peter 2:4-5, *The New English Bible*.

CHAPTER 3

1. *U.S. News and World Report*, February 10, 1986.
2. Mary T. Schmich, "Anxiety Attacks," Chicago *Tribune*, April 28, 1986.
3. Joyce Huggett, "Loneliness," *His*, January 1986.
4. Cheryl Lavin and Laura Kevesh, "Tales From the Front," Chicago *Tribune*, January 1986.
5. *Newsweek*, June 2, 1986, p. 55.
6. "A Slow Coming of Age," *Psychology Today*, July 1986, p. 79.
7. Thomas Kane, *Happy Are You Who Affirm*, Whitinsville, Massachusetts: Affirmation Books, 1980, p. 149.

CHAPTER 4

1. See John 11.
2. David Head, *He Sent Leanness*, New York: The Macmillan Company, 1962, p. 19.
3. *The Book of Common Prayer*, Greenwich, Connecticut: The Seabury Press, 1953.

CHAPTER 5

1. Garrison Keillor, *Lake Wobegon Days*, New York: Viking, 1985, p. 284.
2. Page Smith, *Daughters of the Promised Land*, Boston: Little, Brown and Company, 1970, pp. 314–315.
3. *The New English Bible*.
4. Verses 3-4, *The New English Bible*.

CHAPTER 6

1. January 15, 1986.
2. Luise Eichenbaun and Susie Orbach, *What Do Women Want?* New York: Coward-McCann, Inc., 1983, pp. 52-53.
3. Thomas Kane, *Happy Are You Who Affirm*, Whitinsville, Massachusetts: Affirmation Books, 1980, pp. 110–118.
4. Louis Evely, *That Man Is You*, New York: Paulist Press, 1963, p. 103.
5. Gontron de Poncius, *Kabloona*, Alexandria, Virginia: Time-Life Books, 1941, p. 252.
6. 2 Corinthians 3:18.

CHAPTER 7

1. Psalm 27:13, *New American Standard Bible*.
2. Edith Deen, *Great Women of the Christian Faith*, New York: Harper and Brothers Publishers, 1959, p. 321.
3. *The New Encyclopaedia Britannica*, Chicago: Encyclopaedia Britannica, Inc., vol. 9, 1986, p. 884.
4. Edith Deen, *op. cit.*, pp. 321-322.

5. Deborah Meroff, *Coronation of Glory*, Grand Rapids: Zondervan Publishing House, 1979, p. 75.
6. Sir George Bellew, KCB, KCVO, *Britain's Kings and Queens*, London: Pitkin Pictorials Ltd., 1974, p. 16.
7. *The New Encyclopaedia Britannica*, vol. 5, p. 493.
8. *Selections from the World's Devotional Classics*, New York: Funk & Wagnalls, vol. 9, 1916, pp. 221–222.

CHAPTER 8

1. *Newsweek*, June 2, 1986, p. 45.
2. Maria Nilsen with Paul H. Sheetz, *Malla Moe*, Chicago: Moody Press, 1956, p. 246.
3. *Ibid.*, pp. 25–26.
4. *Ibid.*, p. 29.
5. *Ibid.*, p. 45.
6. *Ibid.*, p. 52.
7. *Ibid.*, p. 93.
8. *Ibid.*, p. 172.
9. *Ibid.*, p. 203.
10. *Ibid.*, p. 214.
11. *Ibid.*, p. 212.
12. *Ibid.*, p. 212.

CHAPTER 9

1. Evelyn Underhill, *The Mystery of Sacrifice*, London: Longmans, Green and Co., 1938, p. 44.
2. Evelyn Underhill, *Light of Christ*, London: Longmans, Green and Co., 1945, pp. 25–26.
3. Isaiah 25:1–2, *The New English Bible*.
4. Isaiah 28:13, *The New English Bible*.
5. Isaiah 30:15–17, *The New English Bible*.
6. G.K. Chesterton, *Orthodoxy*, Garden City, New York: Image Books, 1959, p. 80.
7. *Ibid.*, pp. 10–11, 79.
8. 1 Corinthians 13:12; 2 Corinthians 3:18; James 1:23.
9. John Bunyan, *Pilgrim's Progress*, p. 305.

CHAPTER 10

1. Gregory Stover, "Living With a Live-In Generation," *Good News*, July/August 1986, p. 17.
2. *Christianity Today*, July 11, 1986, p. 28.
3. Chicago *Tribune*, August 20, 1986.
4. Sheldon Vanauken, "Till Someone Else Do Us Part," *Fundamentalist Journal*, June 1984, pp. 40, 48.
5. James 4:2, *The New English Bible*.

6. *The Joseph Parker Treasury of Pastoral Prayers*, Grand Rapids: Baker Book House, 1982, p. 19.

CHAPTER 11

1. Halldor Laxness, *The Fish Can Sing*, New York: Thomas Y. Crowell Company, 1967, p. 103.
2. Jacques Ellul, *The Humiliation of the Word*, Grand Rapids: William B. Eerdmans Publishing Company, 1985, pp. 15, 18.
3. Hebrews 4:12–13, *The New English Bible*.
4. James Gilchrist Lawson, *Deeper Experiences of Famous Christians*, Anderson, Indiana: The Warner Press, 1911, p. 90.
5. Edith Deen, *Great Women of the Christian Faith*, New York: Harper and Brothers Publishers, 1959, p 132.
6. *Ibid.*, p. 136.
7. *Selections From the World's Devotional Classics*, New York: Funk & Wagnalls, vol. 8, 1916, p. 48.
8. Edith Deen, *op. cit.*, p. 131.
9. Thomas à Kempis, *Imitation of Christ*, Grand Rapids: Zondervan Publishing House, 1967, p. 112.
10. *Selections From the World's Devotional Classics*, vol. 8, 1916, p. 83.
11. Calvin Miller, *The Table of Inwardness*, Downers Grove, Illinois: InterVarsity Press, 1984, pp. 111, 118.
12. Hebrews 1:3; Colossians 1:17; Philippians 1:16; John 1:1.
13. Hebrews 4:14–15, *The New English Bible*.

CHAPTER 12

1. Andrew Greeley, *Thy Brother's Wife*, New York: Warner Books, 1982, p. 497.
2. John 13–17.
3. The London *Mail*, August 11, 1985.
4. Robert M. Adams, *The Land and Literature of England*, New York: W.W. Norton & Company, 1983, pp. 311–312.
5. Edith Deen, *Great Women of the Christian Faith*, New York: Harper and Brothers Publishers, 1959, p. 151.
6. Esther T. Barker, *Lady Huntingdon, Whitefield, and the Wesleys*, Claremont, California School of Theology at Claremont, 1984, p. 14.
7. *Ibid.*, p. 43.
8. Edith Deen, *op.cit.*, p. 153.
9. *Ibid.*, p. 153.
10. *Ibid.*, pp. 152–153.
11. Esther T. Barker, *op. cit.*, p. 76.
12. *Ibid.*, p. 101.
13. Edith Deen, *op. cit.*, p. 150.

CHAPTER 13

1. Jonah 2:8, *The Berkeley Bible*.

2. Margaret Clarkson, *Grace Grows Best in Winter*, Grand Rapids: Zondervan Publishing House, 1972, p. 198.
3. Page Smith, *The Nation Comes of Age*, New York: McGraw-Hill Book Company, 1981, p. 659.
4. *Ibid.*, p. 660.
5. *Ibid.*, pp. 650–651.
6. Hugh T. Kerr and John M. Mulder, Editors, *Conversions*, Grand Rapids: William B. Eerdmans Publishing Company, 1983, p. 115.
7. *Ibid.*, p. 116.
8. Page Smith, *op. cit.*, p. 661.
9. *Ibid.*, p. 663.
10. *Ibid.*, p. 660.
11. *The New Encyclopaedia Britannica*, Chicago: Encyclopaedia Britannica, Inc., vol. 12, 1986, p. 9.
12. Habakkuk 3:17-19, *The New English Bible*.

CHAPTER 14

1. Abraham Joshua Heschel, *I Asked for Wonder*, New York: Crossroad, 1985, p. 37.
2. *Ibid.*, p. 36.
3. *Passover Haggadah*, Coffees of Maxwell House, 1981, p. 8.
4. Abraham Joshua Heschel, *op. cit.*, p. 28.
5. Barry Lopez, *Arctic Dreams*, New York: Charles Scribner's Sons, 1986, pp. xxviii, xxix.

CHAPTER 15

1. Lewis Carroll, *Through the Looking Glass and What Alice Found There*, New York: Avenel Books, n.d., p. 194.
2. Daniel Boorstin, *The Discoverers*, New York: Random House, 1983, p. 13.
3. William Shakespeare, *Hamlet*.
4. Daniel Boorstin, *op. cit.*, p. 39.

CHAPTER 16

1. Elizabeth Longford, *Eminent Victorian Women*, New York: Alfred A. Knopf, 1981, p. 87.
2. Edith Deen, *Great Women of the Christian Faith*, New York: Harper and Brothers Publishers, 1959, p. 215.
3. Elizabeth Longford, *op. cit.*, p. 90.
4. *The New Encyclopaedia Britannica*, Chicago: Encyclopaedia Britannica, Inc., vol. 8, 1986, p. 705.
5. Elizabeth Longford, *op. cit.*, p. 101.
6. Elizabeth Longford, *op. cit.*
7. Mary Wilder Tileston, *Joy and Strength*, New York: Grosset & Dunlap, 1901, 1929, p. 44.

CHAPTER 17

1. Chicago *Tribune*, January 11, 1987.
2. Beth Ghiloni, "A Woman's Place! The Velvet Ghetto," *Psychology Today*, September 1984.
3. Susan Fraker, "Why Women Are Not Getting to the Top," *Fortune*, April 16, 1984, pp. 44, 40.
4. Page Smith, *A New Age Now Begins*, New York: McGraw-Hill Book Company, vol. 1, p. 153.
5. Paul Tournier, *The Gift of Feeling*, Atlanta: John Knox Press, 1979, p. 23.
6. Page Smith, *Daughters of the Promised Land*, Boston: Little, Brown and Company, 1970, p. 331.
7. Paul Tournier, *op. cit.*, p. 130.
8. *Ibid.*, p. 100.
9. *Ibid.*, p. 112.
10. Page Smith, *Daughters of the Promised Land*, p. 330.
11. *Ibid.*, pp. 346–347.
12. Paul Tournier, *op. cit.*, pp. 127, 109.
13. *Ibid.*, p. 124.
14. *Ibid.*, p. 130.

CHAPTER 18

1. O'Kelley Whitaker, *Sister Death*, New York: Morehouse-Barlow Co., 1974, p. 31.
2. T.S. Eliot, *The Complete Poems and Plays*, New York: Harcourt, Brace & World, Inc., 1971, p. 145.
3. John 12:32, *The Berkeley Bible*.
4. Ernest Gordon, *A Book of Protestant Saints*, Chicago: Moody Press, 1946, p. 13.
5. *Ibid.*, p. 11.
6. Isaiah 50:10-11, *The New King James Version*.
7. Henri J.M. Nouwen, *The Living Reminder*, New York: The Seabury Press, 1977, p. 25.

CHAPTER 19

1. George MacDonald, *On Tangled Paths*, Wheaton, Illinois: Victor Books, 1987, p. 80.
2. Psalm 106:13-15, *The New King James Version*.
3. Maria Nilsen with Paul H. Sheetz, *Malla Moe*, Chicago: Moody Press, 1956, pp. 252–253.

CHAPTER 20

1. Mary Skinner, *If You Came Here to Live . . .* , Bath, England: Echoes of Service, 1976, p. 12.
2. *Ibid.*, excerpts from chapter 2.

3. Dennis Kinlaw, tape of message given at Asbury College, *The Cross You Must Build in Your Life.*

CHAPTER 21

1. Romans 8:38-39, *The New King James Version.*
2. Proverbs 4:18, *The King James Version.*
3. Hebrews 6:19-20, *The Weymouth New Testament.*
4. C.S. Lewis, *Till We Have Faces*, Grand Rapids: William B. Eerdmans Publishing Company, 1956, p. 294.
5. *Ibid.*, p. 307.
6. *Ibid.*, p. 308.
7. Robin W. Lovin, "Being Unprepared May Be Optimal Holiday Preparation," *Crain's Chicago Business*, December 22, 1986, p. 10.
8. Henri J. M. Nouwen, "Running from What We Desire," *Partnership*, July/August 1986, pp. 34–35.